The Impact of Empire

D1420091

THE SCHOOLS HISTORY PROJECT

S·H·P

OFFICIAL TEXT

THIS IS HISTORY!

The Impact of Empire

MERCHISTON CASTLE
SCHOOL
HISTORY DEPARTMENT

**MICHAEL
RILEY**

**JAMIE
BYROM**

**CHRISTOPHER
CULPIN**

**HODDER
EDUCATION**

Part of Hachette Livre UK

The Schools History Project

Set up in 1972 to bring new life to history for students aged 13–16, the Schools History Project continues to play an innovatory role in secondary history education. From the start, SHP aimed to show how good history has an important contribution to make to the education of a young person. It does this by creating courses and materials which both respect the importance of up-to-date, well-researched history and provide enjoyable learning experiences for students.

Since 1978 the Project has been based at Trinity and All Saints University College Leeds, from where it seeks to support, inspire and challenge teachers through INSET, the annual conference, a biennial Bulletin and the website: http://web.leedstrinity.ac.uk/shp. The Project is also closely involved with government bodies and exam boards in the planning of courses for Key Stage 3, GCSE and A level.

Note: The wording and sentence structure of some written sources have been adapted and simplified to make them accessible to all pupils, while faithfully preserving the sense of the original.

Words printed in SMALL CAPITALS are defined in the glossary on page 140.

The Indian cities of Bombay, Madras and Calcutta are now known as Mumbai, Chennai and Kolkata respectively. Throughout this book we have chosen to use the old names as these were used in the period being studied.

Hachette Livre UK's policy is to use papers that are natural, renewable and recyclable products and made from wood grown in sustainable forests. The logging and manufacturing processes are expected to conform to the environmental regulations of the country of origin.

Orders: please contact Bookpoint Ltd, 130 Milton Park, Abingdon, Oxon OX14 4SB. Telephone: +44 (0)1235 827720. Fax: +44 (0)1235 400454. Lines are open 9.00–5.00, Monday to Saturday, with a 24-hour message answering service. Visit our website at http://www.hoddereducation.co.uk

First published in 2004

This second edition first published 2008

by Hodder Education,
part of Hachette Livre UK
338 Euston Road
London NW1 3BH

Impression number   6 5 4 3 2 1

Year   2012 2011 2010 2009 2008

Cover photo: Topical Press Agency/Getty Images

Illustrations by Art Construction, Peter Bull, Jon Davis (Linden Artists), Richard Duszczak, Tony Randell, Steve Smith, Craig Warwick (Linden Artists)

Typeset in 13pt Goudy by DC Graphic Design Ltd, Swanley Village, Kent.

Printed in Italy

A catalogue record for this title is available from the British Library

ISBN: 978 0 340 95768 4

Teacher's Resource Book ISBN: 978 0 340 96650 1

◆ Contents

SOURCE 1

Look at this picture. You may be wondering why we have chosen to open this book about the British Empire with an everyday, modern British street scene. Be patient. By the end of the book, all will be revealed!

In a street like this today, very few people would think much about the British Empire. But 100 years ago just about every person on any street in Britain would be aware of the power of the EMPIRE and how it shaped their lives. Britain was the greatest power on earth and over a quarter of the world's population lived within its Empire. None of them could ignore its effects.

And now? Some people are still proud of the old British Empire, but accept that it will never return. Others are ashamed of it. But most know very little about it, thinking it is dead and gone, done and dusted.

But is it? This book will try to help you understand that the British Empire still affects our daily lives: who we are, how we live, and what we believe. We hope you will see how the Empire has shaped your world. It may even have shaped your local street! Why not look and see?

The book is divided into three main sections. Between each section you have a chance to pause, and summarise the story so far. The sections are:

◆ **Early empire:** British traders and settlers first move into North America and India
◆ **World empire:** the British Empire grows to the peak of power
◆ **Ending empire:** Britain gives up its control of almost all its overseas lands.

ROANOKE: WHAT WENT WRONG WITH ENGLAND'S FIRST COLONY?

Decide for yourself why it failed

Our history of the British Empire begins in 1585 with this man – Walter Raleigh. Look closely at the portrait and think of three good words to describe Raleigh.

SOURCE 1 A portrait of Sir Walter Raleigh, 1588.

Walter Raleigh was very rich and very powerful. At the beginning of 1585 he was also very excited. For some years he had been the favourite of Queen Elizabeth I. The Queen adored Raleigh and she showered him with gifts of money and property. In the spring of 1585 Raleigh made bold plans for spending some of his vast fortune.

He decided that he would send about 300 English people to live in North America. Raleigh wanted to go down in history as the man who established England's first COLONY. This would be the first English settlement in the unexplored land across the Atlantic Ocean. Nobody in England had attempted anything like this before. Nobody knew whether the plan would succeed.

◆ *Mystery*

In the sixteenth century Europeans knew very little about North America. Spanish merchants had set up trading posts on the islands of the Caribbean (West Indies). They had also conquered the Aztec Empire in central America and destroyed the Inca Empire in Peru. But North America remained much more of a mystery. A few English merchants had sailed across the Atlantic, hoping to make their fortunes by trading with the Native Americans who lived there. They had all returned disappointed.

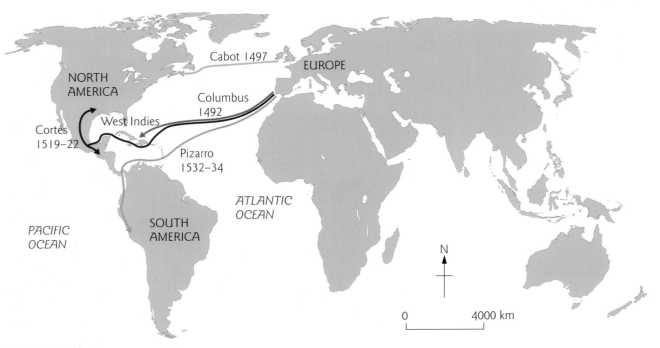

SOURCE 2 European exploration and conquest of the Americas.

Walter Raleigh was fascinated by America. He read everything he could find about the strange people who lived in this 'New World'. He was keen to ensure that his own colonists did not treat the Native Americans as brutally as the Spaniards had done.

In 1584, to discover more about this distant land, and to find a suitable place for England's first colony, Raleigh organised a voyage to America. His men explored the North American coast and found the perfect place – Roanoke.

Roanoke was an island. It was fertile and richly stocked with wildlife. It was sheltered from the Atlantic storms and hidden from Spanish ships by banks of sand dunes. The Native Americans who lived on Roanoke were very friendly towards the strange white people in the big ships. When Raleigh's men returned to England they even brought two Native Americans – Wancheso and Manteo – back to London with them.

YOUR ENQUIRY

In the months that followed, Sir Walter Raleigh made careful preparations to ensure that England's first colony was a success. In fact, the colony was a disaster! In this enquiry you are going to find out why and explain what went wrong.

If you wish: Before you go any further, discuss the things that you think might go wrong. Make a list, then go back to it later to see how right or wrong you were!

◆ The preparations

As Raleigh began to make detailed plans he realised that establishing a colony in America was going to be a huge challenge. It was like taking a whole English village and planting it in an unknown land. Raleigh thought hard about some of the problems he faced.

Raleigh's problems

PROBLEM 1: How will I pay for the colony?

Raleigh's first and greatest problem was how to raise enough money to pay for the ships and supplies. The Queen offered one of her ships, the *Tiger*, and gave Raleigh £400 worth of gunpowder from the Tower of London. But Raleigh needed a lot more than this and he did not want to use up all of his own money.

PROBLEM 3: Who should lead the colony?

Raleigh needed brave and intelligent people to lead his expedition. An experienced commander should lead the voyage.

   A trusted governor should be in charge of setting up the colony. A respected scholar and painter should make a detailed record of the strange people, beasts and plants of the 'New World'.

PROBLEM 2: How can I persuade people to go?

Raleigh needed about 600 people for the voyage. Half of these would stay in America to set up the colony. When Raleigh began recruiting, he found that it was difficult to persuade people to join the voyage. It was particularly hard to find ordinary sailors as many were afraid of being captured and tortured by the Spanish.

PROBLEM 4: What food and supplies will the colony need to get started?

If the colonists were lucky enough to arrive in spring, they would be able to sow their crops. However, they would still need enough food supplies to last them the five months until the crops could be harvested. The colonists would also need to take materials to build a fort. There was no stone near Roanoke and Raleigh wondered if the colonists should take stone from England.

PROBLEM 5: How should we treat the Native Americans?

Roanoke island was already inhabited by Native Americans. They had been friendly to Raleigh's men when they first visited Roanoke but nobody really knew how they would react to people actually coming to live on their land. Raleigh knew that thousands of Aztecs and Incas had lost their lives in the Spanish conquest of their land in Central and South America. He would need to make sure that the English COLONISTS lived on good terms with these Native Americans.

ACTIVITY A

Which of these problems do you think Raleigh was unable to solve by using his money?

Raleigh's solutions

Raleigh was pleased with the solutions he found. But, if you think carefully, you will probably be able to think of some of the things that might go wrong with Raleigh's plans.

SOLUTION 1: paying for the colony

Raleigh decided that he had to persuade English merchants to lend him money to pay for the new colony. He promised the investors a share of the loot from any Spanish ships that could be raided on the way to America. Wealthy merchants soon began to invest in the project.

SOLUTION 2: persuading people to go

Raleigh asked the Queen for sweeping new powers to force men into service on his ships. Elizabeth gave her permission and sailors in the ports of the West Country were forced into service against their will.

SOLUTION 3: choosing the leaders

Raleigh had little trouble finding a commander for his expedition. **Richard Grenville** had two essential qualities: he loved adventure and he hated Spain. However, he also had a fiery temper and a liking for too much good wine. Apart from a short sail across the English Channel, the voyage to America was Richard Grenville's first attempt at seamanship.

The governor of England's first colony was to be **Ralph Lane**, an expert on building forts and a man who enjoyed a hard life.

Raleigh hired **John White**, a talented artist, to record the expedition.

Finally, **Thomas Harriot**, Raleigh's friend from Oxford University, was employed to study and to map the new territory. Harriot was the only person who could communicate with **Wancheso** and **Manteo**, the Native Americans who were returning to Roanoke with the colonists.

SOLUTION 4: food and supplies

Raleigh thought very carefully about the food and supplies (or PROVISIONS) which the new colony would need. Meat, fish, grain and other foods were packed onto the ships with great care so that they would not rot. Large quantities of beer, cider and wine were loaded. Herbs and medicines were carefully packed.

No one knew much about the soils on Roanoke and so a variety of seeds were taken, to be sure that some would grow.

The quantity of provisions was impressive, but it was nowhere near enough. Grenville would have to stop in the Caribbean to stock up on salt, fruit and livestock. This was not going to be easy as every port was controlled by the Spanish who were under strict orders not to sell anything to the English.

SOLUTION 5: avoiding brutality

Raleigh declared that there were to be severe punishments for anyone who:

- hit a Native American
- forced a Native American to work against his or her will
- entered the house of a Native American without his or her permission
- raped a Native American woman.

ACTIVITY B

What a mess! There were so many reasons why the colony at Roanoke might go wrong.

Hang on a minute! Raleigh got a lot right. There were plenty of reasons why the colony at Roanoke stood a good chance of succeeding.

Use the information on these two pages to find reasons to support each of these views.

◆ The voyage to Roanoke

7 Two weeks after leaving Hispaniola the expedition reached the coast of North America. A storm threatened. Even in good weather shallow sandbanks made this stretch of coastline near Roanoke extremely dangerous. Disaster struck. The ships hit a sandbank just as the storm began. For more than two hours the *Tiger* was battered by huge waves. The sailors' lives were spared, but when they hauled the wreck of the *Tiger* onto the beach, their hearts sank. The seawater had ruined nearly all their supplies. The colonists would now have to rely on the Native Americans for food.

ATLANTIC OCEAN

Roanoke Island

NORTH AMERICA

5 When the *Tiger* arrived in Puerto Rico Grenville was bitterly disappointed. Not one of the other English ships had arrived. The tropical heat now ruined what little food was left. The sailors ate biscuits infested with weevil. They drank the water with their teeth clenched to strain out the worms. Many men became sick. To make matters worse they were now in hostile Spanish territory. Fortunately another of the fleet's ships, the *Elizabeth*, soon arrived in Puerto Rico.

6 On 1 June 1585 the *Tiger* and the *Elizabeth* arrived at the island of Hispaniola. This was the colonists' last hope of obtaining food before they reached the North American mainland. Manteo warned the colonists that food was always scarce on Roanoke in winter. It was essential that they obtained animals and seedlings in the Caribbean. Grenville and his men were surprised to find a warm welcome from the Spanish governor of Hispaniola. The governor supplied the colonists with everything they needed, together with large quantities of sugar, ginger and pearls.

PUERTO RICO

HISPANIOLA

CARIBBEAN SEA

N

4 Twenty-one days after leaving England the *Tiger* arrived in the Caribbean. It was now so hot that several of the sailors dived into the surf. This was a terrible mistake. One poor man had his leg bitten off by a shark. He screamed in pain as the stump was dipped in boiling tar to CAUTERISE it.

SOUTH AMERICA

| 0 | 1000 | 2000 | 3000 km |

1 On 9 April Grenville's flagship, the *Tiger*, together with the four other vessels in the fleet, set sail from Plymouth. Grenville was afraid that some sailors on the other four ships might try to steal food and drink. He insisted that nearly all the supplies should be stored on the *Tiger* where he could keep an eye on them. This would turn out to be a serious mistake.

ENGLAND

Plymouth

EUROPE

FRANCE

PORTUGAL

SPAIN

2 Ten days after leaving England the sky darkened and the air turned cold. Grenville and his men experienced a partial eclipse of the sun. On the east coast of America the eclipse was total. The Native Americans saw this as an omen that some great evil would soon arrive at their shores.

AFRICA

CANARY ISLANDS

3 The fleet was approaching the Canary Islands when a violent storm blew up. The ships lost sight of each other. Grenville had already thought of the possibility that the ships might get split up on such a long voyage. He had arranged for them to reassemble on the island of Puerto Rico in the Caribbean.

You have to admit that the colonists had some good luck on the voyage.

Hang on a minute. Most things that went wrong were just bad luck.

ACTIVITY

Think carefully about the events of the voyage. Find examples to support each of these views.

Yes, but they made a lot of mistakes on the voyage too.

◆ First encounters

Grenville planned to settle Raleigh's colonists on Roanoke Island, 100 kilometres to the north of where they had landed.

A few days after the disastrous storm Grenville and his men were overjoyed to see two of their lost ships on the horizon. Most of the scattered fleet was now reunited. Grenville set off with sixty men in four small boats to explore the shallow waters of Pamlico Sound.

Grenville knew that it was essential to make friendly contact with the Native Americans who lived along the shores of Pamlico Sound. It was the only way that the colonists could survive. Over the next week Grenville and his men explored over 300 kilometres of coastline. They visited the three Native American villages of Pomeioc, Aquascogoc and Secotan.

SOURCE 3 The area around Roanoke.

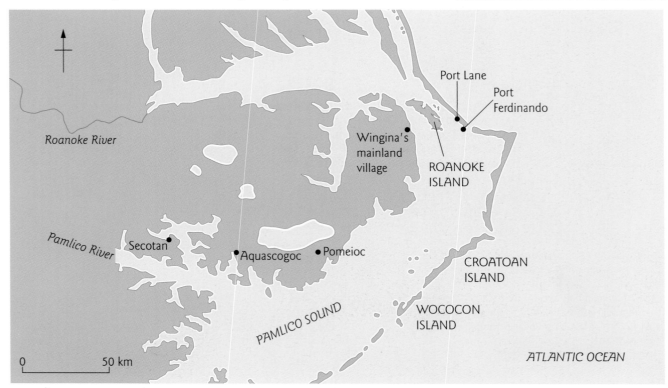

Pomeioc

After a hard day's rowing through the swamps, the colonists landed near the small settlement of Pomeioc. They pulled the boats ashore, picked up their MUSKETS and nervously set off for the village. As the colonists approached Pomeioc they saw longhouses built from rough poles and covered in mats. A group of Native Americans sat around a campfire in the middle of the village.

The colonists were amazed by the appearance of these people. The men wore deerskin around their waists. Their hair was shaven to form a crest on top of their heads. The women also wore deerskin, but did not cover their breasts. They had shaved hair and tattoos on their cheeks.

John White set to work painting this watercolour of a woman and child (Source 4). The child was frightened by John White's beard, but stood still to allow him to paint her when he gave her an English doll.

SOURCE 4 John White's painting of a Native American woman and her child.

ACTIVITY

Look at Source 4.

1 What details of the woman and child's appearance did John White include in his painting?
2 What does the painting suggest about John White's attitude towards the woman and child?

Aquascogoc

It was at the next village, Aquascogoc, that something went dreadfully wrong. The Native Americans here did not seem pleased to see the Englishmen, and so the colonists returned quickly to their boats. It was only later that Grenville noticed that his silver drinking cup was missing. He was furious and sent his men back to the village to have his revenge. The Native Americans had fled, but the Englishmen set fire to the village and to the corn which surrounded it. This was a very hasty and foolish thing to do. After all, the colonists would soon have to depend on the native people for food.

Secotan

The last village the colonists visited was Secotan (see Source 5). The Native Americans here were thought to be hostile, so some of the English wore full armour. They were surprised to be welcomed by a friendly chieftain who arranged an evening of entertainment. The colonists enjoyed the feast. They were amazed by the strange dances which the Native American men and women performed around a circle of posts carved with weird human heads.

Secotan was very similar to Pomeioc, apart from a large building with a barrel-shaped roof. When Thomas Harriot asked to be taken inside he found himself surrounded by mummified corpses. This was the 'charnel house' where the Native Americans mummified the bodies of their dead relatives, in order to preserve them for the after-life.

ACTIVITY

Look at Source 5 on page 13.
1 What details of life in Secotan did John White include in his painting?
2 What does the painting suggest about John White's attitude towards Native Americans?
3 In what ways does White seem to have differed from Grenville in his attitude and behaviour towards the Native Americans?

SOURCE 5 John White's painting of Secotan.

Their rype corne

Their greene corne

Corne newly sprong

Their sitting at meate

The place of Solemne prayer

The house wherin the Tombe of their Herounds standeth

SECOTON

A Ceremony in their prayers &
strange iestures and songes dansing
abowt posts carued on the topps
lyke mens faces.

◆ *The English settlement on Roanoke*

At the end of July 1585, Grenville and his men returned from their expedition around Pamlico Sound. They sailed north to Port Ferdinando where they began to unload supplies for their planned settlement on Roanoke. Grenville knew that the colonists could only settle on the island if the Native Americans agreed. The chief of the local tribes, Chief Wingina, was recovering from a war wound, so Grenville met with the chief's brother. The two men agreed that the colonists should settle on the north-eastern part of Roanoke, near Shallowbag Bay.

Ralph Lane now took up his role as the colony's governor. When all the supplies were unloaded, Lane started the urgent task of building a fort. There was no stone on Roanoke, so Lane was forced to build a fort from a deep ditch, banks of sand and timbers. When the fort was finished, Lane ordered the men to start work on the other buildings. Ralph Lane and the other gentlemen had decent houses, but the rest of the men lived in rough wooden shacks. They then worked on the church, storehouse, armoury, stables and jail. By the third week in August the building work was complete. Grenville set sail for England as planned, leaving 107 colonists behind. This was a smaller number than Raleigh had planned, but more realistic given the shortage of supplies.

The colonists' links with England were now broken. They were totally alone. Their food supplies were very low and they began to fear the future. The colonists began to disagree among themselves. Many did not share Ralph Lane's enjoyment of hardship: there were too many gentlemen who were not used to hard work. Over half the colonists were soldiers and some of these men began to behave badly. Lane punished them harshly. At least one soldier was hanged. His rotting corpse was left hanging from a tree as a warning to others.

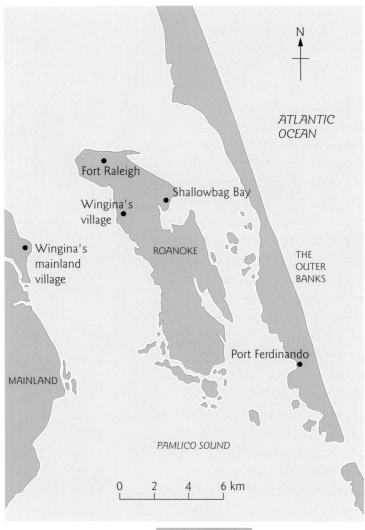

SOURCE 6 A map of Roanoke.

A few weeks later, the colonists received their first visit from Chief Wingina. They were keen to meet this powerful chief, who ruled over all the Native Americans on Roanoke as well as a small settlement on the mainland.

Wingina was wary of the English colonists. He knew that many Native Americans had died shortly after a visit from the Englishmen. Wingina thought that this might be because the colonists had supernatural powers. In fact, some of the colonists were carrying measles and smallpox, and the Native Americans had no immunity to these European diseases. Wingina also knew that the English colonists would be forced to depend on his people for food during the coming winter months: the colonists had arrived at Roanoke too late to plant any seeds; they found it difficult to shoot animals in the forest because so much of their gunpowder was damp; and they were useless at catching fish in the shallow waters of Pamlico Sound.

Through the winter of 1585–86 the bellies of the English settlers ached with hunger. Wingina and his people helped the colonists to set traps to catch fish; they also supplied them with corn, but the Native Americans too were running short of food. Wingina began to lose patience with the colonists.

SOURCE 7   One of John White's paintings. The man is believed to be Chief Wingina.

ACTIVITY

1 What does the painting (Source 7) suggest about John White's attitude towards Chief Wingina?
2 Think carefully about what went wrong when the colonists settled on Roanoke. Find examples to support each of these views:

> I think Ralph Lane was the main reason why the colony failed.

> Hang on! There were lots of other reasons why things went wrong.

◆ A bloody end

The chief decided that there was only one solution – to wipe out the English settlement. Wingina moved his base to the mainland. He then ordered his men to destroy the fish traps they had set for the colonists. With the colonists now weakened, the chief planned his attack on the English fort.

Ralph Lane heard about Wingina's planned attack from a Native American who was friendly to the English colonists. Lane decided to attack first. Just after dawn on 1 June 1586 he led 27 of his men across the water towards Wingina's mainland settlement. He pretended that he simply wanted to talk with Wingina. When Lane and the English soldiers entered the village they saw Wingina and several village elders sitting around the campfire. The soldiers fired their muskets straight into the group of men.

Wingina was the first to be hit. The colonists thought he was dead, but the chief suddenly sprang to his feet and ran into the forest. A band of soldiers set off after him. One of the soldiers caught sight of Wingina and fired his pistol. He hit the chief on the buttocks, but Wingina was not badly injured and he ran on. He had now shaken off all but two of the soldiers, and they were finding it difficult to run through the forest in their heavy clothes.

SOURCE 8 A woodcut showing the attack on Wingina's village.

Ralph Lane waited anxiously in the village. He had no idea whether Wingina was alive or dead. After a long time, the two exhausted soldiers emerged from the forest. Lane saw that one of them was clutching something in his hand – the bloody head of Chief Wingina.

The death of Wingina meant that the English colony was now safe from Native American attack. But good relations between the English settlers and the Native Americans were in ruins. In the end this did not matter to the colonists on Roanoke. Within a few days the settlers would be on their way back home. England's first colony would be abandoned.

The colony abandoned

On 10 June the colonists awoke to a wonderful sight. Twenty-three English ships were anchored off the coast. Sir Francis Drake had brought a fleet of ships to rescue Raleigh's starving colony on Roanoke.

The departure of the colonists from Roanoke was chaotic. Nearly all the charts, notes, maps, specimens, paintings and seeds were dropped in the sea. But these records of the 'New World' were not the only things to be left behind. In the rush to leave before a storm began, Drake's fleet set off for England leaving three of the colonists on the island. What became of these men is a mystery which has never been solved.

So, in 1586, England's first colony ended in failure. In the years that followed other groups of colonists would attempt to settle in America. Eventually they would succeed. During the seventeenth century a string of European colonies would grow up along the east coast of America. And many more Native Americans would die from the white men's diseases and guns.

ACTIVITY

Roanoke failed mainly because the colonists were so poorly prepared. It was doomed from the start.

I disagree. In so many ways the colonists were simply unlucky.

I think you are both missing the point. The main reason Roanoke went wrong was because of the attitude and behaviour of some of the colonists towards the Native Americans.

Think carefully about the end of the colony. Find examples to support each of these views.

FINAL ACTIVITY

The editor of a history magazine has asked you to write an article for the next issue. The title will be, 'What went wrong with England's first colony?' Use the notes that you have made in the activities for this chapter to write the article. You can make your article really good by:

◆ telling the story of Roanoke in an interesting way
◆ giving your own clear explanation of what went wrong
◆ selecting three interesting pictures for your article.

Play the East India Company Trading Game to find out

In 1600, fourteen years after the failure of the Roanoke colony, a group of Tudor merchants started an organisation that was to change the history of the world. They called it the East India Company (EIC). At the time, these men had no idea just how powerful their new company was to become. All they wanted to do was trade with India to make themselves rich.

But, in history, what people intend and what actually happens are often two very different things.

In 1608 the East India Company sent its first ship on the long voyage to India. The London merchants waited eagerly for its return. They hoped that it would be full of fine silks, spices and jewels. They also hoped that its captain, Sir William Hawkins, would have won the friendship of the great Indian ruler, the Mughal emperor. They were to be sadly disappointed.

When the ship finally returned in 1612 the crew reported that . . .

- they had collected very few valuable goods
- rival traders from Portugal had tried to murder Hawkins in India
- Indian officials had taken away all Hawkins' money
- the Mughal emperor had refused to grant special trading rights to the East India Company
- Hawkins had died on board his ship on the way back to England.

It was not a good start.

But within 150 years this same East India Company was making massive fortunes for its members and SHAREHOLDERS. Even more surprisingly, it ruled large parts of the Mughal emperor's lands across India. The men who had set out to become traders in India had become the rulers of India.

SOURCE 1 East India House, the London Headquarters of the East India Company. This engraving was made in 1784.

Your enquiry requires you to work out how and why, after such a poor start, the East India Company ended up as the virtual ruler of huge parts of India. The East India Company (at the time) and many British historians (since) claim that it was more or less an accident that the British ended up taking control of India. See what you think: were the British just traders who became 'accidental rulers' or did they know exactly what they were doing?

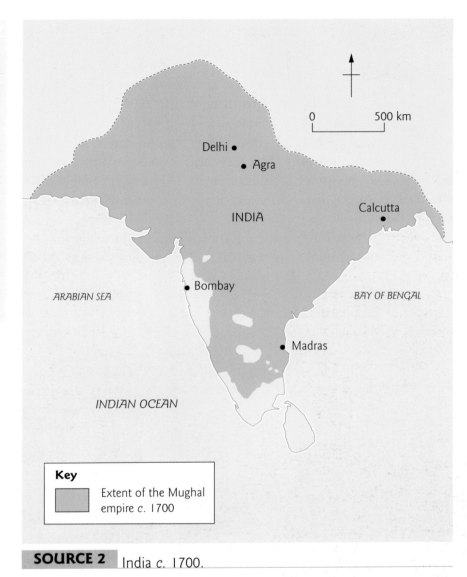

SOURCE 2 India c. 1700.

The EIC governors were not put off by the failure of Sir William Hawkins. They sent other representatives to India who won the right to set up small 'factories' as trading bases.

By 1700 the EIC owned land at three main bases in Madras, Bombay and Calcutta. From these bases, company agents would travel around trading with Indian merchants.

English travellers and traders in India were often impressed by what they saw. In 1679 Thomas Bowrey wrote about his travels in India and praised the country for its skilled craftsmen, able merchants, clever mathematicians, gifted artists and architects. He declared that the Indians were as intelligent as any people on Earth.

By 1700 the EIC had been trading in India for almost a century. From its scattered bases it had established a settled pattern of trade. It had won huge privileges: the merchants paid no taxes and no customs duties. The Company was very wealthy.

By 1700 the Company's trade depended on Aurangzeb, the Mughal emperor (see Source 3). He was a strict and powerful ruler who made the Mughal empire bigger than ever. He always made sure that the officials and princes in each local area stayed loyal to him. While Aurangzeb ruled, the East India Company traders had his protection.

But in 1707 Aurangzeb died. After this no one could keep control in the same way. His sons and grandsons fought each other to take his place while local rulers grabbed power for themselves and turned on each other in a scramble for land and riches.

Over the next half century East India Company agents faced serious problems, as the following activity should show.

SOURCE 3 An eighteenth-century portrait of Aurangzeb.

ACTIVITY

Soon you will play the East India Company Trading Game. But first you need some important information.

Each player takes the part of an East India Company agent. It is 1740. You are about to set off on an eight week journey through southern India, collecting the usual goods.

On your return (in other words when you have finished the game) you must write a report for the EIC directors in London. You must tell them:

◆ what sort of goods you have been trying to collect
◆ what helped you to trade (i.e. events from the game that made it easy to collect goods)
◆ what hindered your trade (i.e. events that made it difficult to collect goods)
◆ why you think the directors should take over areas of India and rule them.
    Explain why this will make trade easier ... but point out how it may cause some problems as well.

Good luck ... you may need it!

How to play the East India Company Trading Game

◆ Play the game in groups of three or four. Each player is a different agent.

◆ The game board is on pages 22–23. You will also need a dice, or six cards numbered one to six, shuffled and placed face down on the table.

◆ There will be eight rounds in the game. Each round represents one week.

◆ In each round you (and all the other players in turn) must:

1 roll the dice (or pick one of the cards)

2 find the correct number on the left-hand side of the board and look across to the correct week to find out what has happened to you

3 record what has happened in a journal, using a chart like the one below. Make sure you include enough details to help you write a really good report afterwards.

calico (cotton cloth)

saltpetre
(for making gunpowder)

spices (e.g. pepper)

Week number	What happened	Goods gained or lost	Total crates so far

◆ When every player has finished Week 8 work out which agent in your group gathered the most crates. Did anyone reach 100?

Afterwards

When you have finished the game, work as a group to discuss what you could put in each of your reports to the East India Company directors. You will find that talking it through together makes it much easier to write a good report.

Use your journals (and the game board) to give you ideas about what made trade easier and what made trade harder.

Remember that your aim is to persuade the East India Company to take more control over large areas of India. Be sure to come up with lots of good reasons for doing this.

silk (for making clothes)

indigo (a type of dye)

precious gems

THE EAST INDIA COM

	week 1	week 2	week 3	week 4
1	War breaks out between rival princes. You cannot trade here.	You use EIC troops to fight for a local prince. He rewards you with 20 crates of silk.	War breaks out between rival princes. You cannot trade here.	French traders have bought all the goods from your regular contact here.
2	You bribe local officials to set up good trade links. You collect 15 crates of calico.	War breaks out between rival princes. You cannot trade here.	A Hindu festival is taking place here for many days. You move on, collecting nothing.	You bribe local officials to help you trade. Gain 15 crates of gems.
3	War breaks out between rival princes. You cannot trade here.	Local princes impose new taxes so you refuse to trade here.	One of your regular contacts has 20 crates of indigo for you.	A deadly disease is affecting this area. You leave straight away.
4	French traders have taken all the best goods here. You collect nothing.	You sign a treaty to support a local prince. He gives you 15 crates of spices.	One of your regular contacts has 15 crates of spices for you.	You admire a Hindu temple to please the local people. Gain 10 crates of silk.
5	You join in a Hindu festival. This pleases local traders. You gain 15 crates of spices.	This is a peaceful area. You trade easily and gain 30 crates of calico.	No one can control the bandits here. They take all the goods you have gained so far.	You sign a treaty to help a prince. You gain 20 crates of calico.
6	One of your regular merchant friends has 20 crates of indigo for you.	War breaks out between rival princes. You cannot trade here.	You use EIC troops to fight for a local prince. His reward is 20 crates of calico.	War breaks out between rival princes. You cannot trade here.

PANY TRADING GAME

week 5	week 6	week 7	week 8
You try to stop a local custom that you think is cruel. No one trades with you.	War breaks out between rival princes. You cannot trade here.	You sign a treaty to help a prince. He rewards you with 20 crates of spices.	War breaks out between rival princes. You cannot trade here.
You pay a high price to outbid rival French traders. Gain 10 crates of gems.	There has been a good harvest. You gain 20 crates of spices.	War breaks out between rival princes. You cannot trade here.	The monsoon season arrives early. You cannot trade in such heavy rain.
War breaks out between rival princes. You cannot trade here.	This is a very peaceful area. You gain 20 crates of indigo.	Landslides block the roads. You cannot trade in these conditions.	This is a peaceful area. You trade easily and gain 30 crates of calico.
You sign a treaty to support a local prince. You gain 20 crates of saltpetre.	War breaks out between rival princes. You cannot trade here.	There has been a good harvest. You gain 20 crates of spices.	Pirates capture the ship that was to collect your goods. You must stop trading.
One of your regular merchant friends has 20 crates of calico for you.	Local princes introduce new taxes so you refuse to trade here.	War breaks out between rival princes. You cannot trade here.	You use EIC troops to fight for a local prince. He gives you 30 crates of spices.
French traders have bought all the goods from your regular contact here.	EIC troops defeat local bandits. You gain 30 crates of calico.	War breaks out between rival princes. You cannot trade here.	You die of cholera ... but only after you have written your report!

EMPIRE BUILDERS: WHAT DO WE THINK OF WOLFE AND CLIVE?

Reach your judgement on these 'heroes of empire'

In the middle of the eighteenth century, Britain and France were the greatest nations on Earth. They had spread their power far beyond Europe in search of trade and wealth. They were rivals in America, India, the Caribbean and at sea all over the globe. In 1756, after years of squabbling, they went to war. It was a war that changed the world.

SOURCE 1 A painting of a sea battle between British and French ships during the Seven Years War.

By 1763 Britain emerged victorious from this 'Seven Years War'. Her success laid the foundations for her world-wide empire. It is not surprising, therefore, that two men whose victories turned the war in Britain's favour became heroes in their homeland. The names of James Wolfe and Robert Clive have been passed down through history as two of Britain's most remarkable empire builders. Source 2 shows how young people were once taught to admire such heroes.

SOURCE 2 An extract from a school history textbook published in 1956.

Every age has its heroes who stir the imagination and shape the lives of ordinary people. For the child in particular, tales of heroism and adventure, of high courage and achievement, are an important and essential part of his development, as well as his first introduction to history.

YOUR ENQUIRY

When we make a hero of someone, we sometimes say we are 'putting them on a pedestal'. A pedestal is a tall column on which statues are placed so that we literally look up to them.

In this enquiry we want you to learn about Wolfe and Clive and decide which of them you would put on a pedestal. Who is the greater hero? Or will you decide to leave the pedestal empty?

To make your decision, you will need to consider each man's story.

◆ You will need to work in two groups.

◆ When you study the life of Wolfe, Group 1 will gather evidence of reasons to show that Wolfe is a hero of the Empire who deserves to be put on the pedestal. Group 2 will do the opposite and try to show why Wolfe does not deserve to be called a hero.

◆ When you study the life of Clive, the roles will be reversed: Group 2 will find reasons to put Clive on the hero's pedestal; Group 1 will find reasons to oppose this.

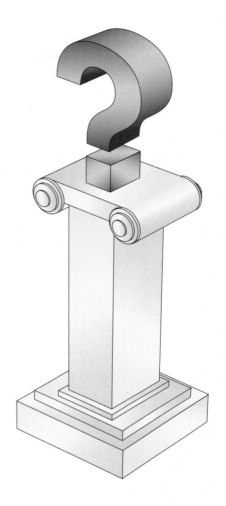

We begin by studying the story of General James Wolfe. In the following section, we deliberately tell the story of Wolfe's attack on Quebec in a way that makes him seem heroic. This should help Group 1. We have also included details of other factors that helped Wolfe. Group 2 could use these to show that heroes need help to make history!

◆ James Wolfe

SOURCE 3 Portrait of Wolfe painted in the 1760s.

Profile

- ◆ Born in Kent in 1727
- ◆ As a young boy Wolfe dreamed of being a great general
- ◆ He was tall, thin and pale with blue eyes and red hair
- ◆ He studied hard, doing extra lessons in subjects he thought would help him become a great general
- ◆ By sixteen he was already an army captain
- ◆ He impressed other officers with his bravery, but took many risks
- ◆ When he was 32 he led the British attack on French armies in North America
- ◆ At 33 he died just after capturing Quebec – the main French base in North America

DISCUSS A

1 Do you think that Wolfe looks like a hero in Source 3?
2 Which three facts from the profile of Wolfe's life would you be sure to use if you wanted to make him appear heroic?
3 Are there any facts that you would definitely leave out?

Rivalry in America

After a false start during Queen Elizabeth's reign, Britain had been able to set up thirteen valuable colonies on the east coast of North America. France had done something similar but, as Source 4 shows, her land ran to the north and west of the thirteen British colonies.

In 1758, during the Seven Years War, the British Prime Minister, William Pitt, decided to try to take Canada from the French. He knew that the key to Canada was the city of Quebec on the St Lawrence River. If the British held Quebec they could stop any supplies coming down the river and the French would have to surrender. The whole war might depend on this one mission. When choosing the man to lead the British against Quebec, Prime Minister Pitt took a risk: he ignored several older officers and turned instead to General James Wolfe.

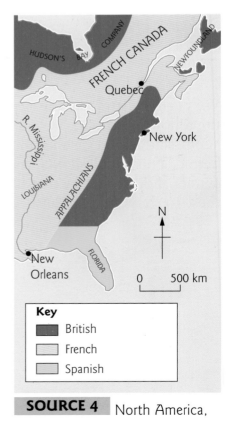

Key

◼ British
◻ French
▨ Spanish

SOURCE 4 North America, 1758.

Mission impossible – the attack on Quebec

The Prime Minister gave Wolfe a force of 8500 men. Wolfe trained the men very hard. He dismissed any soldiers who seemed unfit even though this cut down the size of his army.

In June 1759 the fleet set sail from Britain to Canada. The British ships went further down the narrow, shallow sections of the St Lawrence River than anyone else had ever managed. The navigator was James Cook, who later became another hero of the Empire (but that is another story). Without the navy, Wolfe could not have taken Quebec.

Outnumbered

Quebec stood high above the St Lawrence River. French guns to the east could smash any open attack from across the river, and to the south-west the city was protected by massive cliffs that no army could be expected to climb. The French army was twice the size of the British force. Many generals would have feared that they were doomed to fail. Wolfe did not let that thought cross his mind.

SOURCE 5 Quebec and its defences.

Wolfe ordered British ARTILLERY to pound the city. Quebec suffered terribly – but the French still controlled the river. A French officer sent a mocking message to Wolfe saying, 'You may destroy the town, but you will never get inside it'. Wolfe replied: 'I will take Quebec, even if I must stay until November'.

But time was Wolfe's enemy. The St Lawrence River would turn to ice long before November. Wolfe knew that he had to take Quebec within the next few weeks or his men would freeze to death, trapped in the bitter Canadian winter.

DISCUSS B

What reasons did the French have for thinking Quebec could never be taken?

The Heights of Abraham

Weeks passed and every attack by Wolfe failed. His army was cut to below 7000 by deaths, wounds and sickness. Wolfe himself was very unwell but he told the doctor, 'Patch me up for the work in hand. After that, nothing matters'.

Wolfe's officers wanted to land troops 13 kilometres up the river to the west and to march overland to attack the city. Wolfe finally agreed to attack from the west but invented a more sudden and daring approach: he was going to take 4000 men, at night, up the huge cliffs to the south-west of Quebec. If this plan failed, thousands of his men would die. If it worked, Wolfe would have done his duty for king and country and the British Empire in America would be safe.

On the night of 12 September, Wolfe silently launched his attack. Ships quietly carried 4000 men along the river towards Quebec. Wolfe read his favourite poem to the men as the ships closed in on their landing point.

The ships stopped where Wolfe had spotted a steep, narrow path that zigzagged 60 metres up the cliff face. Wolfe sent an advance party of 150 men up the dangerous path to deal with any French guards. He was lucky: the French officer in charge of guarding the cliffs had sent many of his men away to help with harvesting on nearby farms!

Just before dawn Wolfe's men reached the top of the cliffs and easily overwhelmed the shocked French guards who remained. By 6a.m. Wolfe's full force of 4000 men was in position on the Plains of Abraham above the cliffs. Quebec was barely 2 kilometres away.

As soon as he noticed that Wolfe's men had crossed the river, the French general, Montcalm, managed to gather about 9000 of his men to the Plains of Abraham. At ten o'clock, he ordered them to advance.

Wolfe told his men not to fire until the French were only about 36 metres away. They trusted him and did as he said. They kept their discipline and waited, ignoring the shots from the French. Finally, Wolfe gave the order to fire. The British guns unleashed such a burst of gunfire that the French later described it as being like a blast from a cannon. The British reloaded and fired again. The French were cut to pieces. The British tore into them with bayonets and swords, forcing them to turn and flee.

SOURCE 6   An engraving made in 1759, showing Wolfe's troops climbing the cliffs. Notice that the scale is wrong and that the attack is happening in daylight. Why do you think the artist has done this?

In the early moments of the battle, Wolfe was shot in the wrist but hid his injury with a handkerchief. Then he was hit in the groin by a piece of SHRAPNEL, and finally another bullet hit him in the chest and passed through both his lungs. An officer who was with him described what happened next:

SOURCE 7

'Support me,' cried Wolfe, 'lest my gallant soldiers should see me fall'. But he sank to the ground. He heard a British officer calling out, 'They run! See how they run!'
'Who run?' asked Wolfe.
'The enemy, sir. They give way everywhere!'
Wolfe now knew for certain that Quebec had fallen to the British. He turned on his side and exclaimed, 'God be praised! I now die in peace'.

DISCUSS

Source 8 shows the death of General James Wolfe.
1 Which figure in the painting is James Wolfe?
2 How is Wolfe made to seem heroic in the painting?

SOURCE 8 *The Death of General Wolfe* painted by Benjamin West in 1770.

Consequences of Wolfe's victory

Although it cost him his life, Wolfe's victory at Quebec saved Britain's colonies in North America from falling into French hands. But the story has a twist to it. Things in history are never straightforward!

When the Seven Years War ended in 1763 France gave Canada and other land to the British (see Source 9). At first most people in Britain's Thirteen Colonies were delighted. They hoped to move west and take new land there. But the British government in London said they were not allowed to do this. The government was scared that colonists moving west might start expensive wars with the Native Americans who lived there. To make matters worse, the British Parliament started putting extra taxes on the Thirteen Colonies as a way of paying off some of the huge cost of the war.

Key

- ■ Britain's Thirteen Colonies
- ▨ French land lost to Britain
- ▨ French land given to Spain
- ▨ Spanish land given to Britain

SOURCE 9 North America, 1763.

SOURCE 10 This is what the American flag looked like at the time of the War of Independence.

The colonists were furious! Their anger with the government grew until, in 1776, they finally issued their famous 'Declaration of INDEPENDENCE', saying that London no longer controlled them.

By 1783 the colonists had beaten Britain in a war and the Thirteen Colonies left the British Empire. They gave themselves a new name – The United States of America. Perhaps if Wolfe had failed to take Quebec, the British would never have owned Canada but their empire might have included all the land now owned by the USA. We will never know.

ACTIVITY

Look back through the story of empire builder General James Wolfe (pages 26–31). Group 1 should make a list of reasons to say why Wolfe DOES deserve to be called a hero. Group 2 should make a list of reasons to say why Wolfe DOES NOT deserve to be called a hero.

Now hold a class debate arguing for and against calling Wolfe a hero.

It is time to study our second empire builder as we learn about the extraordinary career of Robert Clive.

◆ Robert Clive

In this section, we tell Clive's story in a way that makes him seem heroic, exactly as we did for James Wolfe. This should help Group 2. We have also included details of other factors that helped Clive and we have shown aspects of his character that are not very appealing! Group 1 could use these to show that heroes need help to make history and that we may not want to put them on a pedestal when we look closely at their character.

SOURCE 11 A portrait of Robert Clive painted in 1770.

Profile

- ◆ Born in Shropshire in 1725
- ◆ As a boy, he was constantly picking fights
- ◆ Local shopkeepers paid Clive to stop him breaking their windows
- ◆ In 1743 Clive's father sent him to India to work for the East India Company (EIC)
- ◆ When the French threatened British trade in India, Clive joined the EIC army and quickly became a general
- ◆ From 1751 Clive won remarkable victories against much larger French and Indian armies
- ◆ After Clive's victories, Indian princes traded with the British and ignored the French
- ◆ In 1757 Clive's army of 3000 men won the Battle of Plassey against 60,000 Indians. He took all the riches of Bengal for the EIC
- ◆ After returning to England, in 1760 Clive became a Member of Parliament and then was made a lord

- ◆ In 1765 he returned to India as the EIC Governor of Calcutta
- ◆ In 1766 Clive went back to England with a fortune of over £3 million. His enemies accused him of corruption (accepting bribes)
- ◆ In 1772–73 Parliament investigated Clive's career and found him not guilty of corruption
- ◆ In 1774 Clive, who was depressed and addicted to opium, committed suicide

DISCUSS A

1 Do you think Robert Clive looks like a hero in Source 11?
2 Which three facts from the profile of Clive's life would you be sure to use if you wanted to make him appear heroic?
3 Are there any facts that you would definitely leave out?

The man of action

As you read in Chapter 2, a group of English merchants started the East India Company in 1600. After a slow start, the Company set up three trading bases at Bombay, Madras and Calcutta.

At first the Company was not interested in taking over any land. Chapter 2 showed you why this changed. In 1707, the death of the Mughal emperor, Aurangzeb, led to a power vacuum. Wars broke out between rival princes. French traders helped the princes win battles and in return the princes promised to trade with the French. Unless the Company did something to stop this, it would be squeezed out of India.

In 1750 British trade in India seemed to be doomed. The French and the Indian princes they supported were on the verge of complete victory. Then Robert Clive entered the story. Just a few years before, he had been so bored with his office work for the East India Company that he had tried to commit suicide, but his gun failed to fire – twice! Only when he joined the Company's army could he show his talents as a man of action.

SOURCE 12 India c. 1740.

In 1751 Clive led a force of 500 British and Indian soldiers and captured an important city called Arcot. He held the city for 50 days against a French and Indian army of 10,000 men. This gave the British time to recover. Over the next four years French power in southern India collapsed. The East India Company emerged as the closest friend and most favoured trading partner of the victorious princes.

DISCUSS B

Look at Source 13. How has the artist made Clive seem heroic in this picture?

SOURCE 13 An artist's reconstruction of Robert Clive at Arcot, from Look and Learn magazine, published in 1967.

Crisis in Bengal

After his success in southern India, Clive returned to Britain as a hero – and as a very wealthy man.

Then, in 1756, a prince in Bengal, in north-west India, dared to attack the East India Company's base in Calcutta. The Company sent Robert Clive to Bengal to teach this prince a lesson.

SOURCE 14 Siraj ud Dowlah, the Indian prince who attacked Calcutta in 1756.

Siraj ud Dowlah had become the nawab (prince) of Bengal early in 1756. He disliked the British taking a bigger and bigger part in his country's trade. Then the British, with their possessions under attack elsewhere in India, fortified their base in Calcutta. This was the last straw for the nawab. He didn't want other nations building forts in his own land. He feared the British were aiming to take over Bengal so he attacked Calcutta.

The story of the 'Black Hole of Calcutta'

When Siraj ud Dowlah attacked the East India Company base in Calcutta, his soldiers held a number of British men and women prisoner overnight, in a room that was about 5 metres by 4 metres with just two small windows.

SOURCE 15 One survivor, John Holwell, later wrote about his experiences:

Of 146 prisoners, 123 were smothered in the Black Hole prison in the night of 20 June 1756 ... From about nine till near eleven ... my legs were almost broke with the weight against them. I travelled over the dead and went to the other end of the room.

Many historians now think that John Holwell greatly exaggerated what happened and some say the event never happened at all. When Robert Clive reached Bengal in 1757, however, he certainly believed all he had been told about the 'Black Hole of Calcutta' and was determined to take full revenge on Siraj ud Dowlah. Clive knew this could be difficult and that he would be heavily outnumbered.

Here is another extract from the school history book from 1956 that started this enquiry. It tells the story of what happened when Clive finally met Siraj ud Dowlah at the Battle of Plassey on 23 June 1757.

SOURCE 16 From *People in History, No. 4, Great People of Modern Times*, by R.J. Unstead.

Clive's army consisted of only about 3000 men while Dowlah faced him with about 60,000. At first Clive decided that it was madness to risk a battle and he must retreat as most of his officers advised. By the next morning however, he had changed his mind and gave the order to advance. The great enemy army broke ranks and fled almost as soon as he attacked, so that the Battle of Plassey, 1757, was one of the most dazzling victories in the history of the world. The British became masters of Bengal, a province larger than the whole of Great Britain.

R.J. Unstead's book certainly makes Clive seem like a hero. See what you think as you look at a few more facts about the battle, and about what Clive had been doing before it started:

▲ Clive's troops were very well trained

▲ The nawab's troops were very disorganised

▲ Clive's army had eight modern six-pounder guns

▲ The nawab's army had 50 heavy cannon

▲ Clive chose a good battleground, giving some cover for his men

▲ Clive used his six-pounder guns well and destroyed the nawab's cannon

▲ Many of the nawab's richest subjects did not like him so Clive plotted with them before the battle. He told them to contact Mir Jafar who was one of the nawab's generals. Clive promised Jafar that he would be made the new ruler of Bengal if he supported the British

▲ When the battle started, Mir Jafar was still with the nawab's army – but he changed sides at the very last minute!

▲ During the battle a violent rainstorm soaked the nawab's ammunition supplies

▲ One of Clive's officers disobeyed him and gave the order to attack at just the right time to turn the battle Clive's way

▲ A lucky shot from a British gun killed the nawab's greatest general

▲ The nawab lost 500 men in the battle. Clive lost 18 men

The painting in Source 17 was made in 1761. By that time Clive had rewarded Mir Jafar by making him the new nawab of Bengal – but the EIC really controlled his lands.

SOURCE 17 Robert Clive meets Mir Jafar after the Battle of Plassey. A painting by Francis Hayman in 1761.

DISCUSS

Look at Source 17.
1 Why do you think the artist has shown both men in the picture?
2 How does the artist suggest that Clive and Britain are more important than Mir Jafar?
3 Some people say this painting looks more like a business deal than a battlefield. What might suggest this?

Consequences of Clive's victory

The Battle of Plassey in 1757 changed the history of the world. Mir Jafar became the new ruler of Bengal, but the East India Company held the real power over the richest area in India. Looking back, we can see that this was the start of the British Empire in India.

Over the next twenty years the Company became more closely involved in Indian politics. In 1765 Clive took over all tax collection in Bengal on behalf of the Company. He – and others – made enormous fortunes in India by bribery, deceit and threats. He said that this was what powerful Indians did and that it was natural that he should follow their example.

Back in Britain, Parliament and the public were ashamed of Clive. In 1772 he was put on trial for corruption. Even though he was not found to be guilty, his reputation never recovered. He became depressed, took drugs and finally killed himself in 1774.

ACTIVITY

Look back through the story of empire builder Robert Clive (pages 32–36). Group 2 should make a list of reasons to say why Clive DOES deserve to be called a hero. Group 1 should make a list of reasons why Clive DOES NOT deserve to be called a hero.

Now hold a class debate arguing for and against calling Clive a hero.

FINAL ACTIVITY

It is time to make up your own mind. Forget about being in Group 1 or Group 2. What do YOU think? Who should go on the pedestal? Should it be:

a) James Wolfe
b) Robert Clive
c) no one?

Whatever you decide you must use facts from the lives of these two extraordinary empire builders to support your case.

4 EMPIRE AND SLAVERY: HOW CAN WE TELL THE STORY OF BRITAIN'S SLAVE TRADE?

Use the evidence to tell two different versions of the slave trade

SOURCE I *The Slave Trade*, a painting by Francois Biard, 1840.

This painting shows a scene on the coast of West Africa in the early nineteenth century. It tells a disturbing story. If you look carefully you will find some shocking details of human misery and suffering.

DISCUSS

What details of human misery and suffering has the artist included in the painting in Source I?

The people in the picture in Source 1 were caught up in one of the most shameful aspects of Britain's colonial history – the slave trade. For over three hundred years European countries forced Africans onto slave ships and transported them across the Atlantic Ocean. The slaves were then worked to death on plantations in North and South America, growing sugar, tobacco and cotton for Europe.

This is part of what is sometimes called 'the triangular trade'.

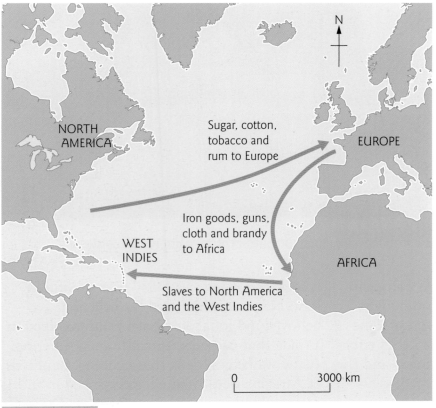

SOURCE 2   The triangular trade.

Europeans did not begin slavery in Africa. For thousands of years slavery had been part of African culture. But the European slave trade was on a different scale. Between 1500 and 1850 more than 11 million Africans arrived on European-owned plantations. Millions more (no one knows the exact figure) died on the journey from their homes to the African coast or on the slave ships as they crossed the Atlantic.

The Portuguese were the first Europeans to trade in African slaves, but other European countries quickly joined in. By the eighteenth century the British were the main slave traders. As the demand for sugar in Britain grew, more and more Africans were taken to the West Indies to work on British sugar plantations.

YOUR ENQUIRY

Slavery is a disturbing part of British history. Many people today are shocked that Britain could have been involved in such a cruel trade. Some people would prefer to forget it completely. However, good historians do not ignore the difficult bits of the past. In this enquiry you will find out about Britain's slave trade and think about the best way to tell this shocking story.

◆ *The journey of the* Duke of Argyle

On a rainy August day in 1750 an old and shabby ship called the *Duke of Argyle* set sail from the port of Liverpool. John Newton, the ship's captain, was starting a fourteen-month journey which would take him to Africa, the West Indies and back to Britain.

Eight weeks after leaving Liverpool, with the West African coast in sight, the crew began to prepare the ship for its cargo – slaves.

For the next six months the *Duke of Argyle* sailed up and down the West African coast, slowly filling its holds with slaves. It worked like this: African traders kidnapped people from villages up to hundreds of kilometres inland. They marched them to the coast where European slave merchants like John Newton bought the slaves. As demand for slaves grew some African kings fought wars against other tribes in order to supply the African traders and the European demand.

By the end of May 1751 the *Duke of Argyle* was packed with slaves. As the ship left Africa for the West Indies, John Newton thought fondly of his wife in England:

SOURCE 3 An eighteenth-century painting of a slave ship.

SOURCE 4 An extract from John Newton's journal.

I have lost sight of Africa. It is now ten in the evening. I am going to walk the deck and think of you and, according to my constant custom, recommend you to the care and protection of God.

It seems strange to us today that a man like John Newton, who loved his wife and believed in God, could have been involved in a trade that caused so much human suffering. As he walked on deck that evening, hundreds of Africans were chained and stacked in the dark and airless holds below his feet. These people had lost their freedom and had been forced from their homeland. Many would never see their families again.

Conditions on slave ships like the *Duke of Argyle* were appalling. The slaves were stacked on shelves sometimes less than a metre apart. They were chained in twos at their hands and feet, making it difficult to move or turn without hurting themselves. When the weather was good the slaves were herded on deck for feeding. In bad weather they were fed below in their filthy quarters. A shared bucket was used as a toilet and this often overflowed in the Atlantic storms. The stink of the slave quarters was unbearable.

It is not surprising that in these conditions large numbers of slaves became sick. The biggest killer was DYSENTERY. This illness was nick-named 'the bloody flux'. Soon after the *Duke of Argyle* left Africa, John Newton began to record the deaths of slaves:

SOURCE 5 An extract from John Newton's journal.

Thursday 23 May ... Buried a man slave (No. 34).
Wednesday 29 May ... Buried a boy slave (No. 86) of a flux.
Wednesday 12 June ... Buried a man slave (No. 84) of a flux, which he had been struggling with near seven weeks.
Thursday 13 June ... This morning buried a woman slave (No. 47). Know not what she died of for she has not been properly alive since she first came on board.

In the 42 days that it took the miserable ship to cross the Atlantic a total of ten slaves died. Their bodies were thrown to the sharks.

The physical and mental suffering of the Atlantic crossing led many Africans into despair. Some became so depressed that they killed themselves by refusing to eat or by jumping overboard if they had the chance. Others were determined to resist.

Just three days into the voyage a young slave, who had been released from his chains because of sickness, managed to push a metal spike through the deck gratings to the slaves below. Within an hour twenty slaves were free. But the sailors had guns and were soon able to regain control. Few slave revolts were successful, but they were common.

At the beginning of July the *Duke of Argyle* approached the West Indies. The crew began to prepare the slaves for arrival. The Africans were taken on deck to be washed. Their holds were cleaned out. This was a likely time for a rebellion so they were exercised in small groups.

On 3 July the ship landed in Antigua. Many of the slaves were very ill. Some died soon after arrival. Those who survived were sold at auction to the highest bidder and taken away to one of the British sugar plantations.

Over the next six weeks John Newton loaded his ship with sugar and headed for home to his wife and family in Liverpool.

ACTIVITY

1 Which of these words would you use to describe John Newton from the evidence on these two pages: cruel, gentle, thoughtful, loving, honest, ruthless, unhappy?

2 We have focused on John Newton, but it took more than just a slave ship captain to make the slave trade work. Make a list of all the other people mentioned on these two pages. Describe their role in running the slave trade.

And . . .

Our aim is to try to give people a rounded and truthful picture of the slave trade. Hidden in this account of John Newton's voyage are other interesting stories which we could have focused on:

Yes, why didn't you focus more on the slave rebellion? It shows that black people resisted slavery.

I think you should focus on Liverpool. Who was paying John Newton? It would show who was really behind the slave trade.

3 Read the account of John Newton's voyage again and then write two or three more speech bubbles each arguing for a different focus on Britain's slave trade.

◆ *Life on the sugar plantations*

The Africans whom John Newton took to the West Indies were bought by British planters. These men owned large sugar plantations on the islands. The planters made huge profits from the sugar trade and they lived in great luxury. On their plantations they not only grew the sugar cane, but also processed the sugar.

Sources 6–8 tell the story of sugar production on the West Indian plantations. Together they give us a very detailed picture of life on the plantations.

ACTIVITY

Look at Sources 6–8 very carefully and answer these questions:
1 What jobs did the following people do on the sugar plantations?

◆ Male slaves
◆ Female slaves
◆ Slave children
◆ White people

2 What made the work on the plantations so hard?
3 What do the pictures tell us about how the slaves were treated on the plantations?
4 These three paintings are by an artist who carefully observed what happened on the plantation. He was paid by the plantation owner who wanted the paintings to hang on the wall of his home in England. How does this affect your judgements in questions 1–3?

SOURCE 6   A print showing slaves working in the sugar cane fields, 1823.

SOURCE 7 A print showing slaves carting the sugar cane to the windmill to be crushed, 1823.

SOURCE 8 A print showing slaves working in the boiling house, 1823.

One problem with the pictures on pages 42–43 is that they all show the same plantation. So we need to ask … how typical was this plantation?

The pictures show only one aspect of life on the plantation – work. So we need to ask … what else happened? What aspects of a slave's life are missing?

Historians have tried to piece together a more detailed and accurate story of life on the sugar plantations using lots of different sources. Here are some of their findings:

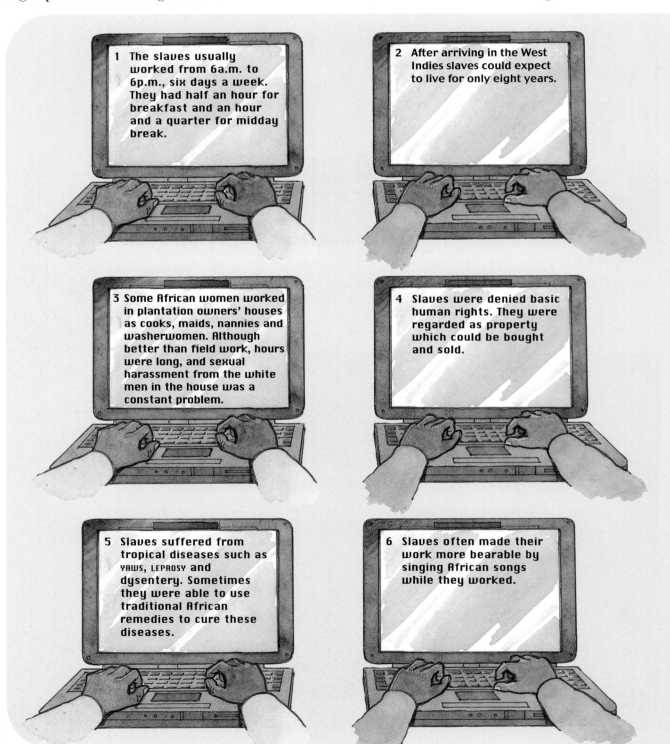

1 The slaves usually worked from 6a.m. to 6p.m., six days a week. They had half an hour for breakfast and an hour and a quarter for midday break.

2 After arriving in the West Indies slaves could expect to live for only eight years.

3 Some African women worked in plantation owners' houses as cooks, maids, nannies and washerwomen. Although better than field work, hours were long, and sexual harassment from the white men in the house was a constant problem.

4 Slaves were denied basic human rights. They were regarded as property which could be bought and sold.

5 Slaves suffered from tropical diseases such as YAWS, LEPROSY and dysentery. Sometimes they were able to use traditional African remedies to cure these diseases.

6 Slaves often made their work more bearable by singing African songs while they worked.

7 Some slaves managed to save money by growing food to sell and by trading their skills.

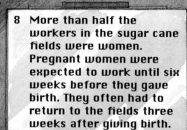

8 More than half the workers in the sugar cane fields were women. Pregnant women were expected to work until six weeks before they gave birth. They often had to return to the fields three weeks after giving birth.

9 British visitors to the West Indies were often surprised to find a rich tradition of African music and dance on the plantations.

10 Slaves who ran away could be given over a hundred lashes. They were sometimes branded on the face or had their ear nailed to a post.

11 Slaves were severely punished in horrible ways. For example, twelve lashes of the whip were given for bad work.

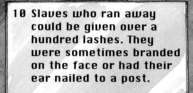

ACTIVITY

Historians still have different points of view about plantation life. Here are two examples:

Dr Doubtful says:

> I want to expose people to the cruelty of slavery. I want to emphasise how brutal life on the plantations really was.

Professor Positive says:

> I want to tell a positive story about plantation life. I want to emphasise how slaves rose above the horrors and were not just victims.

Choose one of these viewpoints; then select which findings (from points 1–11) you can use to support your viewpoint.

◆ Black people in Britain

One of the results of the slave trade was that more black people came to Britain. Africans had been in Britain since Roman times, but it was in the eighteenth century that black people settled in Britain in large numbers. Some were slaves brought to Britain by their masters. Others were former slaves who had been granted their freedom or who had escaped from the plantations.

It is difficult to write about the history of black people in Britain in the eighteenth century because few left a record of their experiences. However, if we search in the sources that we have and think hard, we can begin to tell the stories of Britain's early black communities.

ACTIVITY A

In this activity the action shifts to Britain. But again, our two historians want to tell rather different stories:

Professor Positive

In the eighteenth century we find the beginnings of a strong black community in Britain. Black people played an important part in many aspects of British life and many white people supported the black settlers.

Dr Doubtful

Slavery was part of British life. Here in Britain in the eighteenth century human beings were bought and sold as slaves. Black settlers were EXPLOITED terribly. They had to put up with extreme forms of racism that seem shocking today.

Use Sources 9–13 to gather as much evidence as you can to support **each** story.

SOURCE 9 A painting of the family of Sir William Young painted in 1766. The black servant in the picture is a groom. In other rich households black people worked as gardeners, footmen and maids. During the eighteenth century it became fashionable to include a black servant in family portraits. This was a way in which rich people showed off their wealth.

A fine Negro boy

offered for sale in Liverpool.
Is said to be about 4 ft 5 in. tall. Of a sober, tractable [willing], humane disposition. Eleven or twelve years of age, talks English very well, and can dress hair in a tolerable way.

SOURCE 10 This advertisement for a slave appeared in a Liverpool newspaper called *Williamson's London Advertiser* in 1768.

SOURCE 11 This advertisement for a runaway slave appeared in a London newspaper called the *Public Advertiser* in 1768. Many advertisements like this one appeared in newspapers during the eighteenth century.

Run away from his master, a Negro boy, under five feet in height, about 16 years old, named Charles. He is very ill made, being remarkably bow-legged, hollow-backed and pot-bellied. He had on, when he went away, a coarse dark brown linen coat, a thick waistcoat, very dirty leather breeches and on his head an old velvet cap.

Whoever will bring him, or give any news of him, to Mr Beckford in Pall Mall, will be handsomely rewarded.

SOURCE 12 In 1771, James Somerset, a black slave in London, escaped from his master Charles Stewart. Somerset went into hiding in London's black community, but his master found him, placed him in chains and tried to send him back to the West Indies. Somerset's friends managed to bring his case to court. The judge, Lord Mansfield, ordered Somerset to be freed because, although slavery was still legal in Britain, slaves could not be taken from Britain by force.

This report of the celebrations in the black community appeared in the *Public Advertiser* in June 1772:

On Monday near 200 Blacks, with their ladies, had an entertainment at a public house in Westminster, to celebrate the triumph which their brother Somerset had obtained over Mr Stewart, his master. Lord Mansfield's health was echoed round the room and the evening was concluded with a ball. The tickets for admittance to this black assembly were 5s each.

ACTIVITY B

Work in pairs. One of you is Professor Positive, one is Dr Doubtful. You are being interviewed for a TV programme about attitudes towards black people in Britain in the past.

Choose three of the sources on pages 46–47. For each of the sources you have chosen, explain how it supports your overall argument.

SOURCE 13 This is a portrait of Ignatius Sancho. It was painted in 1768 by Thomas Gainsborough, one of the leading artists of the time. Sancho was a famous black writer and musician who owned a shop in London. He was born on a slave ship heading for Grenada. While Sancho was still a small child his mother died and his father killed himself rather than be a slave. Sancho came to London as a child and eventually became butler to the Duke of Montague. Sancho soon taught himself to read and write. In 1773 he married Anne, a black woman, and opened a grocery shop in Westminster. Sancho had many friends among London's artistic community. His compilation of letters became a best-seller when it was published as a book in 1782.

REVIEW 1 RULE BRITANNIA
Play Mix and Match to
summarise two hundred years of empire

In 1740 a grand party was held in an English country house. The guest of honour was the Prince of Wales. As part of the entertainment, a choir performed a new song. You will know the chorus.

Rule Britannia!
Britannia rule the waves.
Britons never, never, never shall be slaves.

You probably also know the figure of Britannia. In early images she is usually shown wearing long robes, holding a spear and sitting by the open sea. The image became popular in the seventeenth century after the British navy defeated their great rivals, the Dutch. Soon Britannia appeared on many British coins. By the late eighteenth century her spear had changed to a trident – the sign of power over the seas. Britain was sure she ruled the waves!

The places in red on the map below show the British Empire in 1783. The first four chapters in this book have shown how Britain gained many of these overseas possessions, which were mostly distant islands and coastal ports. This is why Britain's navy was so important; it protected merchant ships as they carried goods around the world. If Britain could not rule the waves, it could not build an empire.

SOURCE 1 The British Empire in 1783.

ACTIVITY A

The list below summarises the development of the British Empire between 1585 and 1783. Match each letter on the map with one of the places in **bold print**.

◆ **Roanoke** – where Walter Raleigh's first attempt to start a British colony failed in 1586 (see pages 4–17). Others succeeded later (see page 26).

◆ **Madras, Bombay and Calcutta** – where British merchants in India set up their first trading bases by 1700. They sent ships back to Britain filled with tea, spices, silk and other goods from the Far East (see page 19).

◆ **Bengal** – taken from Indian princes by Robert Clive after the Battle of Plassey in 1757, after which it was ruled by the British East India Company (see pages 32–36).

◆ **Quebec** – which General James Wolfe took from the French in 1759, gaining Canada for Britain (see pages 26–31).

◆ **The thirteen North American colonies** – that declared independence from the British Empire in 1776, ruling themselves as the 'United States of America' from 1783 (see page 31).

◆ **The West Indies** – where African slaves grew sugar and other crops on British plantations (see pages 38–47). In **Britain**, some families used the profits from the sugar trade to build grand country houses.

◆ **West African coastal bases** – such as **Gambia** supported the British trade in African slaves to the West Indies (see pages 38–40). Some Africans were taken back to Britain to work as servants for rich families. Others became sailors on British ships. By 1783, thousands worked in British ports and cities (see pages 46–47).

SOURCE 2 A British coin showing Britannia and her trident.

ACTIVITY B

Link each of these statements to one or more of the developments listed in Activity A.
By 1783 ...

◆ Tea had become a hugely popular drink in Britain
◆ Britain believed she was a great world power
◆ Thousands of black men and women lived in Britain
◆ William Shakespeare (*The Tempest*), Daniel Defoe (*Robinson Crusoe*) and Jonathan Swift (*Gulliver's Travels*) wrote famous works about travel to unknown lands
◆ Many black people living in Britain suffered from racism
◆ The British loved sweet foods, and suffered problems with tooth decay
◆ Many country mansions were built in the late eighteenth century
◆ English was the language spoken in the United States of America
◆ Curry appeared in London restaurants as early as 1773
◆ Thousands of British jobs were linked to trade with the colonies

DISCUSS

Do any of these developments still affect life in Britain today?

5 CONVICT COLONY: WHAT MAKES A GOOD HISTORICAL FILM?

Plan your own movie

You probably recognise this place – Sydney harbour, Australia. Even though Australia is on the other side of the world it is a country that seems very familiar to us. We speak the same language, play the same sports and watch some of the same television programmes. We might even have friends or relatives who live in Australia.

In the eighteenth century Europeans knew hardly anything about Australia. In 1770 Captain James Cook and his crew sailed their ship, the *Endeavour*, along part of the eastern coast of Australia, where Sydney now stands. Cook and his men were disappointed by the barren landscape. They collected some strange plants and creatures, but left after a few days. For seventeen years after Cook's voyage no other Europeans went to this vast, unknown land.

Then, in 1787, the British government made an extraordinary decision. For many years criminals had been transported across the seas as an alternative to being hanged or imprisoned in England. At first they were sent to America, where they were forced to work for plantation owners. But by 1787 America was no longer part of the British Empire, and English prisons had begun to overflow. The government decided to turn the newly discovered continent of Australia into a vast jail!

The man in Source 1 was chosen to lead the first convict fleet and to govern the new colony. His name was Captain Arthur Phillip. During the winter and spring of 1787 Phillip prepared for the voyage. He bought the eleven small ships that would make the long journey to Australia and organised all the other supplies that would be needed.

The first convicts arrived, chained together and shivering, in the open wagons that carried them to Portsmouth. Few of these people were dangerous criminals. James Grace, an eleven-year-old boy, had simply stolen some ribbon and a pair of silk stockings.

SOURCE 1 A portrait of Captain Arthur Phillip.

The convicts were herded on board the ships. Their quarters had no portholes, and candles were banned because of the risk of fire. By May 1787 nearly 1500 people – officers, seamen, marines and convicts – were crammed onto the ships. They then began the long and terrifying journey beyond the seas.

SOURCE 2 The route of the First Fleet's journey to Australia, 1787–88.

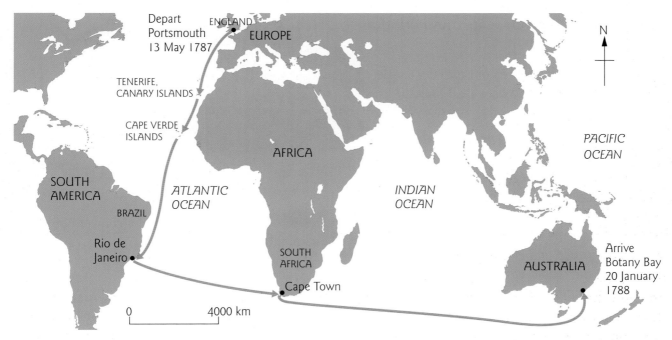

Depart Portsmouth 13 May 1787

ENGLAND
EUROPE

TENERIFE, CANARY ISLANDS

CAPE VERDE ISLANDS

AFRICA

SOUTH AMERICA

ATLANTIC OCEAN

BRAZIL

Rio de Janeiro

SOUTH AFRICA

Cape Town

INDIAN OCEAN

PACIFIC OCEAN

AUSTRALIA

Arrive Botany Bay 20 January 1788

N

0   4000 km

Source 2 shows the 24,000-kilometre journey that the First Fleet made to Australia. You can see that Phillip took an indirect route in order to pick up supplies and to take advantage of the winds and currents. At first the voyage went well, but in the tropics the crew and convicts were plagued with rats, bedbugs, lice, fleas and cockroaches. The BILGES sloshed with a mixture of urine, vomit, dung and dead rats.

After leaving Cape Town the convict quarters became more crowded than ever because the convicts had to make room for the farm animals which Phillip bought for the new colony. On 19 January 1788 the crew on Phillip's flagship, the *Sirius*, finally saw the coast of Australia – eight months after leaving England!

Phillip's fleet anchored in what would later become Sydney harbour. In his journal Phillip described it as 'the finest harbour in the world'. It was here, in the weeks that followed, that Britain's convict colony was built. Between the years 1787 and 1868 more than 160,000 convicts were transported from England and Ireland to Australia.

SOURCE 3 The *Sirius*, flagship of the First Fleet, at anchor in Sydney harbour.

YOUR ENQUIRY

In this enquiry you will make plans for a film about Britain's convict colony in Australia. You will need to use your imagination to select key events, interesting characters and exciting locations to keep viewers interested. You will also have to make sure that your film is as historically accurate as possible.

◆ The criminals

Thomas Holden was a weaver from Bolton, Lancashire. In 1812 he was involved in forming an early trade union to fight for the rights of weavers. For this 'crime' Thomas was sentenced to seven years transportation.

SOURCE 4 From his cell in Lancaster Castle, Holden wrote this letter to his wife, Molly:

Dear Wife,
It is with sorrow that I have to tell you that today, at my trial, I received the hard sentence of seven years transportation beyond the seas. If I was to be in prison I would try and content myself, but to be sent from my native country, perhaps never to see it again, distresses me beyond comprehension. To part with my dear wife and child, parents and friends, to be cut off in the bloom of my youth without doing any wrong to any person on earth – oh my hard fate! May God have mercy on me.
Your affectionate husband until death.
Thomas

Thomas Holden could not bear to be separated from his wife and child. Other letters have survived in which he pleaded with Molly to raise the money for her passage to Australia. She did not.

Thomas was soon taken from Lancaster Castle to the south coast of England. The journey lasted eight days. He travelled in an open cart with other men, women and children. The convicts were heavily chained and dressed in rags. They had no protection from the rain or from the taunts of the people they passed on the road.

For the next five months Thomas Holden was imprisoned on a hulk like the one you can see in Source 5. The hulks were old warships, left to rot and used as prisons in the ports of southern England. They were cramped, wet, dark and vile-smelling places. New convicts were forced to hand over all

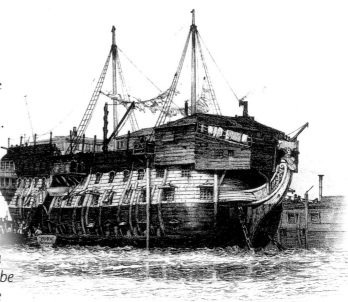

SOURCE 5 An engraving of a convict hulk at Portsmouth, 1828.

their possessions. A heavy iron was fastened to their right ankle. The convicts were then ready to work from dawn until dusk on the government dockyards. The hulks were brutal places. Even small children were placed in irons. Flogging was common. Female convicts were often raped.

◆ The voyage

By the 1820s most convict ships took about four months to reach Australia, making only one stop, at Rio de Janeiro in South America. Today, it is hard for us to imagine the suffering that people faced on such a long and difficult journey. About two hundred convicts were crammed into the holds of a converted merchant ship. Four convicts shared a wooden BERTH 2 metres square. There was less than 2 metres headroom. The only air came from the hatchways, which were covered with heavy iron grilles and were heavily padlocked. In the blazing heat of the tropics the PITCH melted and burned the convicts' flesh as it dripped from the timbers.

Once the ships were in open sea the convicts' leg-irons were removed. However, their bunks were fixed with irons so that they could be chained up if they misbehaved. For serious offences, such as mutiny, convicts would be brought on deck, tied to a grating and given 50 lashes with a CAT O' NINE TAILS. The prisoners and the ship's company watched the painful flogging in silence. It is not surprising that there were few mutinies on the convict ships.

The ship's surgeon tried to make sure that as many prisoners as possible survived the journey. He issued lime-juice each day to protect the convicts from SCURVY. Whenever possible, he brought the convicts on deck for fresh air and exercise. Convicts complained about the 'salted horse meat' which they were sometimes given to eat. In the tropical heat, two pints of warm, dirty water a day left the convicts thirsting for more. But at least the surgeon made sure that each person had enough food and water to stay alive. After 1815, only one convict in a hundred died on the voyage to Australia.

SOURCE 6 A nineteenth-century painting of a convict ship.

ACTIVITY

Use these headings to write the plan for the first part of your film, which will look at the transportation of the convicts to Australia.

Characters
Make Thomas Holden your main character, but decide on three or four other characters who will be introduced in the first part of your film. Use your background knowledge and imagination to write short character sketches about each of your characters. Make sure you explain how each character was involved in transportation.

Events and locations
Use your background knowledge and imagination to work out a sequence of five or six events and their locations, which will form the story in the first part of your film. For example, your first event and location might be:

Event	Location
Thomas Holden is sentenced to seven years transportation	The court room in Lancaster Castle

Historical accuracy
A really good film will need to be historically accurate. Make a list of up to five important ideas about the system of transportation which you want people to understand in the first part of your film.

In order to make your film really accurate there will be lots of questions about the system of transportation and daily life at that time which you will need to research. Make a list of these questions for your team of researchers.

◆ *The convict colony*

The second part of your film will cover Thomas Holden's life at the convict colony. The pictures and information in this section should give you lots of ideas about how your story might develop.

Source 7 shows a picture of Sydney harbour painted 33 years after the first convicts landed. You can see how much the area developed in that time.

SOURCE 7 A painting of Sydney harbour in 1821.

D I S C U S S   A

1 What does Source 7 tell us about life in the convict colony in 1821?
2 In what ways has the artist made Sydney seem a pleasant place to live?

On the left of the picture in Source 7 you can see a group of convicts quarrying stone. All the convicts who arrived in Sydney faced several years of hard labour. At night they were locked up in the convict barracks, but during the day they dug ditches, felled trees, planted crops, put up buildings and built roads. If they were lucky they might find themselves working as a labourer for one of the free settlers who had come to farm in the colony. All convicts were expected to work for ten hours a day from Monday to Friday and for six hours on Saturday. If they worked more hours than this they were paid for the extra work – either in money or in rum.

To the west of Sydney, in the distance, were the Blue Mountains. In 1813 three settlers found a way across this huge mountain range and were amazed by the rich, golden grassland on the other side. In the years that followed, difficult convicts were sent to build roads over the Blue Mountains. Life in a 'road gang' like the one in Source 8 was terrible. Day after day convicts broke stones and shovelled earth with heavy irons biting into their legs. They spent the freezing nights in prison huts on wheels, which they dragged behind them as the road was made.

SOURCE 8 A road gang on the Great West Road across the Blue Mountains, painted by Augustus Earle, 1826.

D I S C U S S   B

1 What does Source 8 tell us about the road gangs?
2 What aspects of life in a road gang are not shown in this picture?

Britain's PENAL colony in Australia was based on harsh punishment. Source 9 shows one of the most common forms of punishment – flogging. Convicts who broke the colony's rules were given 25, 50 or as many as 100 lashes. Even 25 lashes was a terrible torture which skinned a man's back and left it a tangled web of knotted scars. Men who were able to stand up to a flogging in silence were known as 'pebbles' or 'iron men'. A man who cried and screamed was called a 'sandstone' because he was said to crumble like the rock around Sydney harbour. There were always more 'sandstones' than 'pebbles'.

SOURCE 9 An engraving of a convict being flogged, 1836.

SOURCE 10 The first Australian railway, painted c. 1840.

Source 10 shows the first version of a railway in the convict colony. As you can see, it was powered by male convicts. Obviously, these men could not be kept in leg irons and this made it quite easy for a convict to escape. Escaping was easy; the hard thing was to survive. Some convicts took to the sea in stolen boats or on home-made rafts. A lucky few might be picked up by a merchant ship in need of more crew, but most drowned.

Other convicts, kown as 'bushrangers', ran off into the BUSH. They kept themselves alive by catching wild animals or by stealing from travellers and Aborigines. Few escaped convicts survived for very long in the harsh environment of the Australian bush.

The place that convicts feared more than any other was Van Diemen's Land – the island, now called Tasmania, which lies to the south of Australia.

Macquarie Harbour, Van Diemen's Land, was the wettest and most windswept place in Australia. The ferocious sea made escape impossible. It was here that the most troublesome convicts were sent. They lived in the cold barracks on Sarah Island, off the coast of Van Diemen's Land. At 6a.m. each morning they were herded onto boats and taken to the mainland to cut down the huge pine trees in the forests around the harbour. The convicts at Macquarie Harbour worked twelve hours a day in winter and sixteen hours in summer. Most of the time they were half-starved and chilled to the bone. If they broke an axe or insulted a guard, they were taken to Grummet Island. No convict could land here without being soaked, so they had to sleep naked or in wet clothes, without a fire or a blanket.

Source 11 shows convicts towing a raft of pine logs to the sawmill at Sarah Island. To the right is Grummet Island with the punishment hut. You can see the dark opening in the rock where prisoners who misbehaved were kept in solitary confinement.

SOURCE 11 A sketch of Macquarie Harbour, Van Diemen's Land, by T.J. Lempriere, 1830.

ACTIVITY

You now need to plan the second part of your film based on Thomas Holden's life in the convict colony.

Characters
Write brief character sketches for three or four new characters who will appear in the second part of your film.

Events and location
Use your background knowledge and imagination to work out a sequence of four or five events and locations that will form the story in the second part of your film.

Historical accuracy
◆ Make a list of up to five important ideas about the convict colony which you want people to understand in the second part of your film.
◆ Think of some good questions about life in the convict colony for your team of researchers.

◆ The Aborigines

From what you have read so far, you might think that Australia was an empty land when Britain set up the penal colony. Of course, this was not the case. When James Cook landed in Australia in 1770 the island was inhabited by around 300,000 native Australians – Aborigines. It is now time to bring the Aborigines into the plans for your film.

The Aborigines had lived in Australia for thousands of years before white people arrived on their shores. Aborigines live in hundreds of different tribes, each tribe sharing a particular language and occupying the territory where their ancestors lived. The area around Sydney was the ancestral home of the Iora tribe. The information on this page summarises the Iora's lifestyle and beliefs.

The Iora lived by the coast and their main diet was fish. The women of the tribe twisted fishing lines from pounded bark fibre and made hooks from shells. The Iora fished from canoes which they made from bark.

The Aborigines were not farmers. They did not plant crops or grow fruit and vegetables. Iora women gathered plants from the wild.

Too many children would have made it impossible for the Iora to move around and therefore to survive. A woman could only carry one child as well as food and implements. To avoid having large families the Iora caused abortions by giving pregnant women herbal medicines. If this failed they killed the unwanted child at birth.

Sometimes the men hunted animals on land using fire-sticks, stone axes and spears. They threw their spears with great accuracy and power. They had not invented the bow and arrow, but they were very skilful in tracking and stalking animals.

The Iora, like all Aborigines, were very spiritual people. They had no churches or temples. Instead, every hill, tree, stream and animal had spiritual meaning. The Iora did not believe that anyone could own the land, but if their territory was taken away it would mean a spiritual death.

The Iora never washed. They spent their lives coated in a mixture of fish oil, animal grease, sand, dust and sweat.

In order to survive, the tribe wandered easily over a wide area, feeding as they went. For this reason they could not have permanent houses. Instead, they lived in sandstone caves or in quickly-made bark shelters.

DISCUSS

Look at the information on this page carefully and then think of three reasons why some white people in the eighteenth century might have thought that the Aborigines were inferior people.

'Warra, warra!' These were the first words spoken by the Aborigines to the British in Australia. They mean 'go away'. But the British did not go away. When the First Fleet landed in 1788 two Iora tribesmen threw spears which landed wide of the white soldiers. One soldier fired a blank cartridge and the Iora ran away.

At first there was little violence between the white people and the Aborigines. Arthur Phillip gave strict orders that the Aborigines should not be harmed in any way. This continued to be the official policy of the British government in the years that followed.

The British government did not deliberately set out to kill the Aborigines. But the white settlement in Australia destroyed the Aborigines' way of life. Cholera and influenza germs from the convict ships soon infected the native Australians. Rum, which soldiers and convicts in the colony drank in huge amounts, ruined the lives of many Aborigines. On the shores around Sydney white people soon outnumbered Aborigines. The Iora began to die in huge numbers.

DISCUSS

1 Explain what is happening in each of the pictures on the notice in Source 12.
2 What message did the governor want to give to the Aborigines?

SOURCE 12 A notice that the governor of the convict colony produced for the Aborigines in 1828.

From the very beginning of the colony, there was conflict between the convicts and the Aborigines. Convicts stole the Aborigines' weapons to sell as souvenirs. The white prisoners thought of the Aborigines as savages because they could not understand their way of life. They hated the fact that if a convict managed to escape it was often the Aborigines who tracked him down and returned him to the colonial authorities. The convicts came to see the Aborigines as pests who could be killed without hesitation.

As Britain's convict colony grew, kangaroos and other native animals were driven out to make room for sheep and cows. Fences blocked ancient routes. Forests were cut down. Native plants died out. In these ways the Aborigines' way of life was destroyed. The British government declared that all Australia belonged to the Crown. It argued that the Aborigines had no rights over the land because they simply wandered over it. This policy forced the Aborigines off their own land. By the 1830s Iora families, dressed in English rags and drunk on English rum, were a common sight around Sydney (see Source 13).

SOURCE 13 Aborigines on the edge of Sydney, from a painting by Augustus Earle, 1830.

ACTIVITY

You need to think of a way to include the Aborigines in your film. Look again at your ideas about characters, events and locations in the second part of your film. Write a paragraph to explain how you will build the Aborigines into your storyline.

◆ Make a list of five important ideas about the Aborigines which you want the audience to understand.
◆ Think of some good questions about the Aborigines for your team of researchers.

FINAL ACTIVITY

A Hollywood producer has decided he wants to make your film, but he needs to raise the money to pay for it. He wants you to make a trailer for the film to show to the 'money men'. Choose one scene from each of the three parts of the film that you have worked on (Transportation, The Convict Colony and The Aborigines). Briefly describe what should go into each scene so that it shows the most important features.

6

HIDDEN HISTORIES: WHAT CAN LITTLE-KNOWN STORIES TELL US ABOUT BRITISH INDIA?

Draw a graph to show changing relationships in India

◆ The story of Thomas Coryate

This is Thomas Coryate. You have probably never heard of him. He is not very famous and he did little to change history (except that he was the man who introduced the fork to Britain's dining tables!). He is typical of many people or events from the past whose little-known stories often remain hidden from history books.

But Coryate did live a fascinating life. He was the son of a Somerset vicar and served for a while as a jester at the court of King James I. He then surprised everyone by setting off on long walking tours of Europe and beyond. In 1612 he set off on his final and longest journey – to India.

SOURCE 1 A seventeenth-century engraving showing Thomas Coryate.

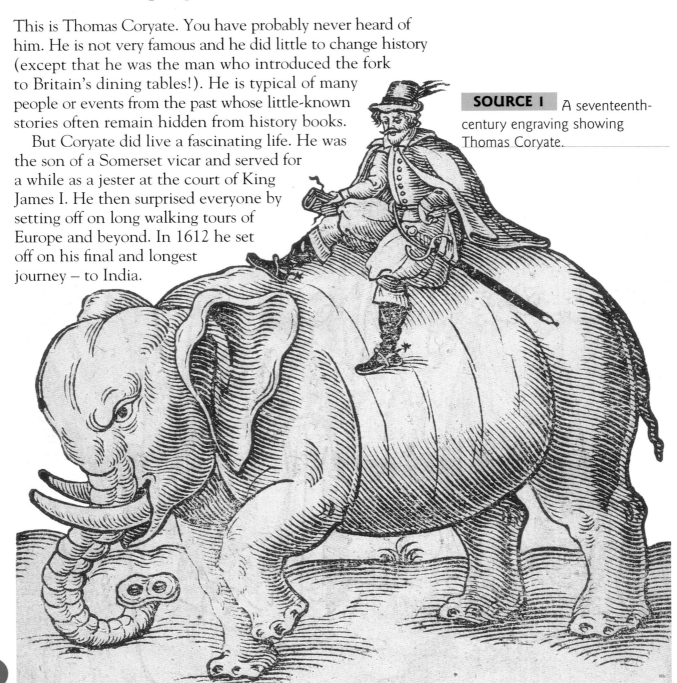

When Coryate reached India in 1615, he visited the court of the mighty Mughal emperor, Jahangir. The emperor had recently allowed Englishmen to trade in his lands and so Coryate's arrival was not entirely surprising. The emperor was rather puzzled by his strange visitor but gave him a few minutes of his time, lent him some money and then ignored him. Even when Coryate preached Christianity from the MINARET of a mosque, the emperor did nothing. He – and many others – thought Coryate was slightly mad but harmless.

No one would pretend that Thomas Coryate was of great importance in history, but historians still love to find out about people like him. His story is fascinating in itself but it can also be used to sum up something far bigger. His odd ramblings through India can be used to sum up just how insignificant and harmless the British were to life in India at the start of the seventeenth century. As time went by, the Indians discovered that the British were to be anything but insignificant in the history of their country!

YOUR ENQUIRY

In this enquiry you will use little-known stories to sum up changes in the relationship between the British and the Indians between 1800 and 1897. In each case you will need to make a 'summary sheet' which tells the main points of the story very simply and makes clear what it shows about the bigger picture. (To help you, we have already done a summary sheet about Thomas Coryate's story as an example.) At the end of the enquiry you will take all your summaries and use them to make a display that tells the bigger story of a century of change.

The story of Thomas Coryate		What the story tells us
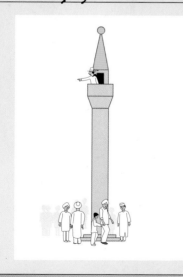	Coryate was an Englishman who was a jester at the court of King James I of England. He travelled on foot around India in 1612. He found out about Indian customs and preached Christianity. The Indians thought he was mad.	Coryate's story symbolises the way in which the first British visitors to India seemed to pose no threat to the Indian way of life. The English just seemed a little odd and the Indians were prepared to welcome them to their country, and then ignore them for most of the time.

◆ The story of the Prime Minister's granny

Thomas Coryate may not have been famous or powerful but this man certainly was. This is Lord Liverpool. He lived 200 years later than Coryate and was the British Prime Minister from 1812 to 1827. History books mention many of his achievements, but there is one fact about him that very few textbooks include. If you read on you will find out about his 'hidden history' and what it symbolises about Britain's relationship with India.

SOURCE 2 A portrait of Lord Liverpool painted in 1827.

Britain's trade with India was just beginning when Thomas Coryate was alive. In the 200 years that followed, much changed. The British East India Company fought wars against Indian princes who made trade difficult. In 1757 General Robert Clive won the Battle of Plassey (see Chapter 3) which gave the British control over India's richest region, Bengal. More and more British traders, soldiers and officials settled in India.

Despite great differences between them, the British and the Indians generally mixed well together at first. Quite a few British traders and soldiers had wives or partners who were Indian. One British general was famous for parading around Calcutta with his thirteen Indian wives, each mounted on the back of a different elephant!

SOURCE 3 A rich and powerful East India Company trader called William Palmer. He is pictured with two of his Indian wives, three of his children and three other women. Palmer was of mixed Indian and British heritage. There were many such families in the trading cities of Calcutta, Madras and Bombay. This picture was painted in 1786.

DISCUSS A

What does Source 3 suggest about William Palmer's attitude towards his family?

One of the many Englishmen who mixed freely with the Indians in the eighteenth century was William Watts. He was an East India Company official who worked as a sort of secret agent before the Battle of Plassey in 1757. Acting on behalf of Robert Clive, Watts made a treaty with a powerful Indian prince called Mir Jafar. The deal was that Mir Jafar would not use his troops against the British in the battle. As a result, the British won the battle and conquered the rich province of Bengal. In return, the British gave Mir Jafar power over much of Bengal.

Watts lived in Calcutta and was married to an Indian woman. In 1750 they had a daughter, Amelia, who later married into the rich and powerful Jenkinson family. In 1812 Amelia's only son, Robert Jenkinson, became … you've guessed it: Lord Liverpool, Prime Minister of Britain. The surprising fact that in 1812 Britain had a Prime Minister who had an Indian granny is another little piece of 'hidden history'.

SOURCE 4 William Watts and Mir Jafar making the agreement.

DISCUSS B

Look back at the picture of Lord Liverpool on page 62. Can you see anything to suggest that his grandmother was Indian?

The story of Lord Liverpool's granny shows how close Britain and India had become by the end of the eighteenth century. They traded together, they made treaties, they married each other. Some British men even followed the Indian custom of having several wives. Neither the British nor the Indians objected. Each race seemed happy to accept the other's way of life despite their differences. But that was to change, as we will see.

ACTIVITY

Make a summary sheet about Lord Liverpool. Use the one on page 61 as an example. Make sure that your sheet has the main heading, *The story of the Prime Minister's granny*. In the first column sum up the main facts about Lord Liverpool – who he was, what his link was to India, etc. In column 2, explain what this piece of hidden history tells us about relationships between British people and Indians in the late eighteenth century.

◆ *The statue's story*

In 1997 the statue in Source 5 was set up in Bristol. It commemorates a remarkable man who died in the city in 1833. His story involves religion, superstition, determination and death. It is not well known, but it tells about a really significant change in the way the British ruled India in the early nineteenth century.

'Live and let live'

When the British first came to India they marvelled at its main religion, Hinduism. Over thousands of years the Indians had developed many religious customs and practices that must have seemed strange or alarming to the British.

Before 1800, British traders were happy to accept or ignore these customs no matter how odd they seemed. After all, they were East India Company merchants. They were traders, not rulers. It might have caused problems among the Indians they traded with if they had tried to interfere. On the whole they decided that it would be best to 'live and let live'. But around 1800 that attitude began to change.

SOURCE 5 Statue of Rammohan Roy on College Green, Bristol.

Challenging the culture

The evangelicals were a powerful group of Christians. They took their Christian faith very seriously. They did not believe in 'live and let live'. They believed they should try to convert people of other faiths to Christianity.

One famous evangelical was William Carey. He was sure that God wanted him to go to India to convert people to Christianity. He arrived in Calcutta in 1793.

At first, British leaders in India – including some bishops – were angry that Carey had come to India. They were scared that he might upset Indian traders by interfering in Hindu beliefs. In fact, Carey won the respect of most Indians. Over the next 40 years, he treated them with great love and respect while challenging some of their customs.

SOURCE 6 A portrait of William Carey.

Sati

In 1811 a deeply religious Indian called Rammohan Roy attended the funeral of his brother in West Bengal. Roy and his family were Hindus. The body was to be burned according to Hindu custom.

The body was carried forward. Then another figure appeared through the crowd. It was the dead man's widow. She was frightened – but she knew her duty. She allowed herself to be tied to her dead husband's corpse.

Roy begged his sister-in-law not to go through with this ancient Indian custom, but the other relatives forced him back. They believed her suicide would show her love for her husband – and would help to pay for any sins her husband had committed. Roy watched as the widow was placed on the bonfire alongside her husband's dead body. She choked and screamed as the smoke and flames enveloped her. She burned alive. The relatives danced around the fire singing 'Maha sati! Maha sati!' (A great wife! A great wife!)

From that day on Roy made up his mind to end this Hindu custom of widow burning, or 'sati' as it was known. He knew that very few of his fellow Indians would help him. He also knew that until recently he could have expected no assistance from the British. But the evangelicals had changed that.

Rammohan Roy became a close friend of Carey, the evangelicals' leader. Together they worked hard to try to end the practice of sati.

In 1829 Roy made a brave decision: he agreed to travel to Britain to try to persuade more British people to support a ban on sati. Some Hindus warned him that travelling overseas would harm his soul forever. Roy dismissed this idea and set sail.

By the end of that year, the British Governor General of India finally decided that the time had come to act. He banned sati throughout British lands in India.

SOURCE 7 A widow committing sati. This picture was painted *c.*1800.

Roy was delighted at this news … but he was *very* unusual. The vast majority of Indians were angry and alarmed. This was a turning point in British rule in India. It was the first time the British had ever used their power to change an Indian custom. Where would it end?

Rammohan Roy died in Bristol in 1833. He is now celebrated in India as a great reformer – but at the time he seemed to have betrayed India by supporting Britain's new desire to interfere with Hindu customs.

ACTIVITY

Make a summary sheet (see page 61) about the story of Rammohan Roy and what it tells us.

◆ The hedge's story

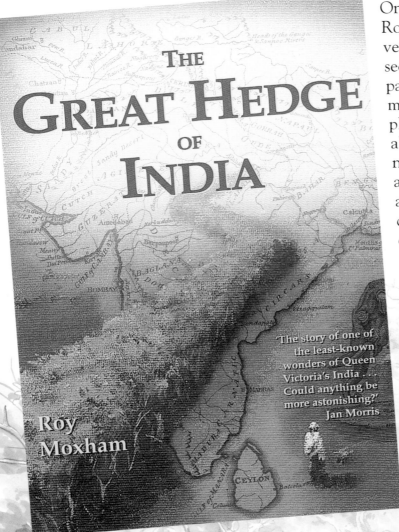

SOURCE 8 Front cover of *The Great Hedge of India* by Roy Moxham.

One day in 1995 a museum worker, Roy Moxham, was browsing through a very old book that he had found in a second-hand shop in London. On one page he read a curious footnote which mentioned that the British had once planted a hedge in India that was almost 2500 kilometres long. He had never heard of this. Other books about India never mentioned it at all. People who knew India well doubted whether this hedge had ever really existed.

But Moxham was hooked: he spent three years following up that one small footnote and wrote a remarkable book (Source 8). The story that he uncovered tells us a lot about how British rule in India was changing by the 1840s.

By 1845 the East India Company controlled huge areas of India. Wherever they went they built roads, bridges and even railways. After banning sati, they also introduced more laws based on Christian standards, and in order to enforce these they had to take charge of law and order and run law courts. All this cost money.

The East India Company made sure that most of the profits from their trade with India went back to Britain. They organised taxes which made it easy for British merchants to sell their goods (such as cotton cloth from the factories of Manchester) in India because Indian businesses could not compete. Britain grew in wealth while huge areas of India remained poor.

The British wanted to raise more money to pay for the cost of governing their land in India – without taking it from their trading profits. They already collected taxes from landowners but they wanted more. They decided to make the most of a way of raising money that rulers in India had used for hundreds of years ... the salt tax.

Salt is really important in hot climates. Quite apart from making food taste better, it gives essential minerals to the body. Rulers in India knew that they could make money by taxing salt since everyone, rich and poor, needed it. The British, however, raised the salt tax to a far higher level than Indians had ever known before. What is more, the British were determined to make sure that everyone paid the tax. This is where the hedge comes in.

Although the British controlled much of India, there were still many independent 'princely states' which did not follow British rule and had different laws and different taxes (see Source 9). In these areas salt was often far cheaper than it was in British-held lands. Naturally, some Indians realised that they could make a huge profit if they could smuggle cheap salt from these states into British areas and sell it there.

In the 1840s the British planted a hedge where the worst salt smuggling took place. Its tough, sharp thorn bushes could tear the flesh of any smuggler who tried to break through it. It ran for thousands of kilometres and was about four metres high and up to five metres thick. It was like a symbol of the British determination to enforce their laws ... and of the division between the old and new ways of ruling India.

Some historians believe that it was wrong of the British to make the Indians pay far higher taxes than Indian princes ever did. People died because they could not afford the salt. Other historians insist that the British used the money to build roads and canals, and to keep law and order. One way or another, more and more Indians must have resented their British masters in a way that would not have happened if they had just been trading partners.

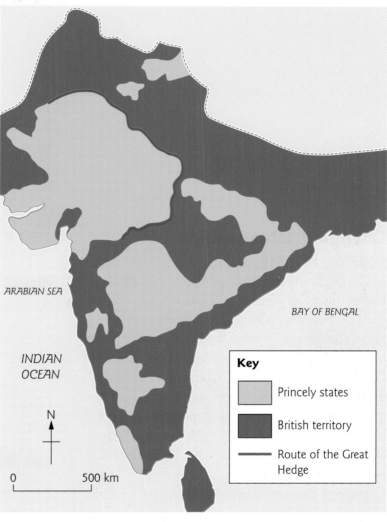

SOURCE 9 Map of India in 1856, showing the princely states and the Great Hedge.

ARABIAN SEA

BAY OF BENGAL

INDIAN OCEAN

N

0   500 km

Key

Princely states

British territory

Route of the Great Hedge

ACTIVITY

Make a summary sheet (see page 61) about the story of the Great Hedge and what it tells us.

◆ *The memsahib's story*

In the early years of the nineteenth century, more and more British women sailed out to India to join their husbands there and raise a family. The Indians called their rulers 'sahibs' and called British wives or daughters 'memsahibs'.

Our next hidden history concerns one of these memsahibs, a young girl we know only as Miss Williams. She grew up in a home very like the one in Source 10, only to meet a shocking death in the blood-stained waters of an Indian river.

DISCUSS A

Compare Source 10 with Source 3 on page 62. How are they different?

Changing relationships

In 1857 Miss Williams lived with her older sister and parents at Cawnpore in northern India. Her father was a colonel in the East India Company's army. Many memsahibs were the wives or daughters of army officers.

Senior officers in the army were always British but most of the soldiers were Indians. They were known as sepoys. There had been a long tradition that the sepoys were proud to serve the British and were loyal to their commanding officers. But by 1857 that was beginning to change.

Part of the problem was that the British officers spent less time with their troops now that their wives were in India. There were other problems too. Sepoy pay had been cut and many sepoys believed that the British were going to force them to drop their Hindu or Muslim beliefs and become Christians. Strains were appearing between the sepoys and their British officers.

In 1857 one Englishman wrote home about how the British were introducing new

SOURCE 10 An engraving of an army officer and his memsahib at breakfast, made in 1842.

laws to change Indian customs and to take land from Indians. He had lived in India for many years and noted that:

SOURCE 11

If a man who left this country thirty years ago were to visit now he would scarcely credit the changes he would see in the treatment of the natives, high and low. The English were not then absolute masters everywhere. Now they are, restraint is cast away ... and they display a supercilious arrogance and contempt of the people.

Of course, a young memsahib like Miss Williams probably knew nothing of these tensions ... until the awful horrors of 1857.

Revolt!

In 1857, some sepoys near Delhi murdered their officers and sparked off a revolt that spread rapidly across the whole of northern India. The violence lasted for almost a year. For a while it seemed that Britain might lose control.

The revolt led to cruelty on both sides. Some of the worst atrocities happened in June 1857 at Cawnpore. Rebels besieged the British army garrison there. Inside were quite a few sepoys who had remained loyal to the British, about 200 British soldiers and many hundreds of women and children. Among these was young Miss Williams.

Day by day, Miss Williams watched as people around her died through wounds, hunger or thirst. Her father was killed early on in the siege. Her mother was shot in the face and took two days to die. Miss Williams was wounded by a bullet in the shoulder but lived to face new horrors.

At the end of June the garrison surrendered. The rebel leader said the British could leave the city by river. But as the unarmed British boarded their boats the fighting broke out once again. The river ran red with blood. Over 250 people were killed. A survivor recorded what happened to Miss Williams:

SOURCE 12

I tell you only what we saw … children were stabbed and thrown into the river. The schoolgirls were burned to death. I saw their clothes and hair catch fire. In the water a few paces off, by the next boat, we saw the youngest daughter of Colonel Williams. A sepoy was going to kill her with his bayonet. She said, 'My father was always kind to sepoys'. He turned away, and just then a villager struck her on the head with his club and she fell into the water.

Miss Williams died in the river. Perhaps she was lucky. The 200 survivors who were recaptured were later hacked to death by local butchers, despite the attempts of some rebel sepoys to protect them.

DISCUSS B

Can you find any signs from the story of the massacre at Cawnpore that the relationship between the British and the Indians had not completely broken down?

SOURCE 13 A nineteenth-century British painting of the massacre on the river at Cawnpore.

Revenge!

The British called the revolt 'The Indian Mutiny', suggesting that the problems were just within the army. In fact many local princes joined in, especially those who had recently lost land to the British. Maybe they saw this as a chance to get rid of the British for ever. Many Indian historians call the revolt a war of independence. It was certainly long, complicated and violent. As this cartoon from *Punch* (Source 14) shows, the British believed justice was on their side.

SOURCE 14 'Justice', a cartoon from *Punch* magazine, September 1857.

DISCUSS

How does Source 14 show that the British believed justice was on their side when they crushed the revolt in India?

In fact, British troops often went beyond the search for justice. They wanted revenge. At Cawnpore they arrested anyone they believed to be a rebel and made them lick the floor where the British had been butchered. They tied some rebels to the mouth of a cannon and blew their bodies to pieces. They knew that cows were sacred to Hindus and pigs were unclean to Muslims so they force-fed Hindu rebels with beef and Muslims with pork before hanging them. Others were simply shot by firing squads.

By late 1858 the rebellion was finally over. Law and order had been re-established. But many thousands had died – including young Miss Williams. The British and the Indians had both committed dreadful crimes. Their relationship would never be the same again.

ACTIVITY

Make a summary sheet (see page 61) about the story of Miss Williams, the young memsahib, and what it tells us.

◆ *The MP's story*

The mutiny failed but it changed India for ever. On 1 November 1858 a proclamation was read out at every railway station in India: the East India Company was abolished and India was to be ruled directly by the British Parliament. All rebels who had not murdered Europeans were pardoned and all Indian religions and ancient customs would be respected. The announcement was followed by a grand firework display.

This was the start of the period known as the 'British Raj'. It lasted from 1858 to 1947. The Indian word 'raj' means 'rule'. Under the British Raj, Queen Victoria was the ruler of all British-held lands in India. (She took the title 'Empress of India' in 1877.) She was represented in India by a viceroy who governed over 300 million Indians, rich and poor, with the help of about 5000 British officials. The army carried on using Indian troops – but it now included far more soldiers from Britain to make sure that there was no repeat of the mutiny.

SOURCE 15 Lord Mayo, the viceroy from 1869 to 1872, summed up the attitude of most British officials in India when he said:

We are all British gentlemen engaged in the magnificent work of governing an inferior [lower] race.

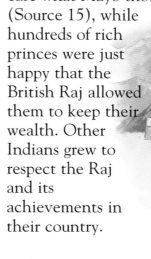

Millions of poor Indians probably did not care what Mayo thought (Source 15), while hundreds of rich princes were just happy that the British Raj allowed them to keep their wealth. Other Indians grew to respect the Raj and its achievements in their country.

However, there were some who were insulted by the attitudes of men like Lord Mayo. Among them was Dadabhai Naoroji (Source 16), another remarkable man whose story is little known in Britain.

Dadabhai was educated at an Indian college run by the British. In 1855 he sailed to England to help run a business there. In London he quickly realised just how little the British people knew about their empire. He decided that it was his duty to educate them. He organised meetings and made speeches about the British Raj. In 1871 Dadabhai made a list of the benefits and failures of British rule in India.

Here are his conclusions:

SOURCE 16 A photograph of Dadabhai Naoroji taken in 1890.

	The benefits of British rule for India:	The failures of British rule:
Humanity	Abolition of sati and of infanticide (the mass killing of unwanted children). Destruction of criminal gangs. Charitable aids in times of famine.	Nothing. Everything is in your favour under this heading.
Civilisation	Education, though yet only partial, is a great blessing. It leads gradually to the destruction of superstition and many evils.	There has been a failure to do as much as could have been done.
Government	Peace and order. Freedom of speech and liberty of the press. Equal justice (but sometimes favouring Europeans). Good service of highly educated administrators.	Repeated breach of pledges to give the natives a fair and reasonable share in running their own country. There is an utter disregard of the feelings and views of the natives.
Wealth	Railways and irrigation. Development of a few valuable products, such as indigo, tea, coffee, silk, etc. Increase of exports. Telegraphs.	Devising new taxes without any effort to improve the people's ability to pay. The great mass of the poor have hardly two pence a day and a few rags. There have been famines that the British could have prevented. There has been a loss of manufacturing industry and skill.

DISCUSS

Look at the table above.

1 What does Naoroji like most about what the British have done in India?
2 What does Naoroji like least about the British in India?
3 How might the British people respond to his views?

Dadabhai did more than just make speeches and write leaflets. Back in India in 1885, he helped to set up the Indian National Congress. This was an organisation that was full of well-educated Indians who were loyal to Queen Victoria. They did not want to end British rule, but they did want responsible Indians – such as themselves – to be given important posts in the government of their own country. The British ignored their demands.

In 1886 Dadabhai returned to England with an extraordinary ambition: he wanted to become a Member of Parliament in Britain. You might imagine that English voters would never choose as an MP someone who dared to criticise the Raj … but you would be wrong. In 1892 Dadabhai won the seat of Central Finsbury in north London by just six votes. He became the first ever Indian Member of Parliament at Westminster.

ACTIVITY

Make a summary sheet (see page 61) of Dadabhai Naoroji's story and what it tells us.

SOURCE 17 This picture shows the House of Commons in 1893. Somewhere amongst all those white, British faces must be the one Indian who had won the right to speak for the millions of people in his country whose lives were ruled by decisions made by this Parliament. Another example of hidden history!

FINAL ACTIVITY

1 Prepare a **large** display graph based on the one shown here. Place each summary sheet where you think it belongs on the graph. You will need to find the right date and then decide how good or bad the relationship between the British and the Indians was at that time.

2 Underneath the graph write a paragraph explaining how the relationship between the Indians and the British changed during this period.

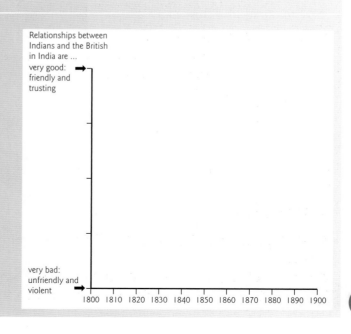

Relationships between Indians and the British in India are …

very good: friendly and trusting

very bad: unfriendly and violent

1800 1810 1820 1830 1840 1850 1860 1870 1880 1890 1900

7

OUT OF AFRICA: WHO SHOULD HAVE THE BENIN HEAD?

Trace the history of the bronze head and decide where it belongs now

If this head could talk it would tell you a very disturbing story
    ... of fear and greed,
    ... of honour and broken promises,
    ... of violence and revenge.
The head would also tell you a lot about one of the most astonishing episodes in the history of the world: the so-called 'Scramble for Africa'.

SOURCE 1   The Benin head, from the Royal Albert Memorial Museum in Exeter.

YOUR ENQUIRY

This bronze head is now in a museum in Exeter. Through this enquiry you will trace the story of the head: where it came from and how it ended up in Exeter. At the end you will decide who should have it now – the people of Britain or the people of Benin, where the head came from originally.

As you make up your mind about the Benin head, you will see how the impact of empire building long ago is still being felt in surprising disputes and arguments facing us today.

◆ The 'dark continent'

The story of how the bronze head came from Benin to Exeter begins long ago, in the fifteenth century.

Ships from Europe first sailed down the west coast of Africa in the 1480s. The Europeans set up trading bases and ports. Their ships took on supplies or cargoes of slaves. But these Europeans did not go far inland to explore or to settle. They knew little or nothing about magnificent African kingdoms, such as Benin.

If they had ventured into Africa they would have found:

- ◆ cities and towns
- ◆ powerful kings
- ◆ large empires
- ◆ trade over long distances
- ◆ skilful craftspeople – working in bronze, ivory and wood.

The rulers of Benin were called Obas. They were powerful men, in total control of a remarkable kingdom in west Africa.

The people of Benin believed that the Oba was descended from the god who made the world. Only the Oba could carry out important religious rituals, such as the one which ensured that there was a good harvest. In these rituals the Oba was accompanied by elaborately dressed attendants carrying shields and swords.

Craftspeople made fine objects for the Oba to wear in the religious rituals, or at his court. They worked in ivory (from elephant tusks), wood, coral (imported from far away on the other side of Africa), brass and bronze. The bronze heads such as the one shown in Source 1 were made after the death of an Oba. Each one was decorated with ivory, beads, wooden rattles and bells, and put on an altar. It was intended as a permanent and precious reminder of the Oba who had died.

In the years after 1700, the empire of Benin lost much of its land. But its customs, art, religion and the importance of the Obas carried on much as before. These remained unseen and undisturbed by Europeans, who thought of Africa as the 'dark continent'. Then everything changed, in twenty frantic years at the end of the nineteenth century.

DISCUSS

In the 1700s the Europeans called inland Africa the 'dark continent'. What do you think they meant?

◆ *The Scramble for Africa*

By 1880 the British, French and Portuguese had taken over some coastal areas of Africa, but only a few explorers, such as David Livingstone, had travelled far inland. Then, in an extraordinary burst of activity from 1880 to 1900, almost all of Africa was carved up between Europe's leading nations. This has become known as the 'Scramble for Africa'. You can see its effects by comparing Sources 2 and 3.

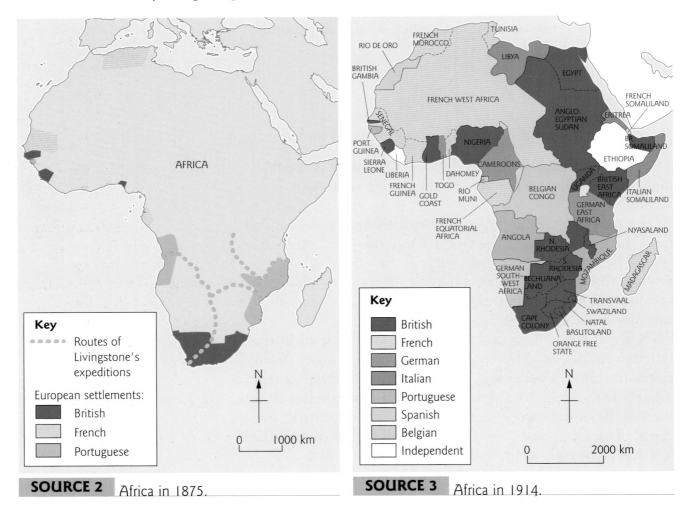

SOURCE 2 Africa in 1875.

SOURCE 3 Africa in 1914.

There is no single reason why European powers started taking African land in such a hurry after 1880. Often they believed it would help their trade. Sometimes they guessed the land might be rich in minerals such as gold or diamonds. Sometimes they hoped that the land would be good for farming.

It reached the point when nations grabbed land just to keep up with others. The King of Belgium took a huge area around the Congo River, saying 'I did not want to miss the chance of getting a piece of this African cake.'

All sorts of people took part in the Scramble for Africa. Match these descriptions to the people in the picture on the right.

◆ **Missionaries** went to spread the Christian faith, to heal the sick and to end certain African customs.
◆ **Explorers** went in search of adventure and new knowledge.
◆ **Traders** went to collect crops and minerals from the heart of Africa – and to find new customers.
◆ **Officials and soldiers** went to protect trade routes so that profits kept flowing.
◆ **Politicians** wanted to please their people by increasing national wealth and pride.

In reality, some people mixed several of these roles: for example, a soldier might have been a keen Christian, or a missionary might also have needed to be an explorer.

SOURCE 4 An African war scene, 1879.

No one seemed to consider what the African people thought as their lands were carved up by foreigners. The Europeans drew new boundaries that sometimes split ancient tribal areas. If the Africans tried to fight, European weapons and technology could usually crush their resistance easily (see Source 4).

Over time, Europeans worked hard to improve healthcare and education in many parts of Africa. However, in these early years most Africans were deeply alarmed by the newcomers. One chief, King Mwanga, complained that 'the English have come … they have built a fort, they eat my land, and yet they have given me nothing at all.' He was not the only African leader to suffer at the hands of the English … the Oba of Benin had a similar experience in 1897.

ACTIVITY

Write a short, simple description of what happened between 1880 and 1900 and to explain why you think the events of these years became known as the 'Scramble for Africa'. Try to use words and phrases that capture the idea of a **scramble**!

◆ *The Benin massacre*

Now that you know about the Scramble for Africa, you can make more sense of the next stages in the story of the bronze head of Benin.

ACTIVITY

Choose one of the following characters and as the story is read out listen for what your character does, fails to do, or says. At the end you will think about the ways your character may have helped to cause what eventually happened.

◆ The Oba of Benin
◆ Captain Gallwey
◆ Ralph Moor
◆ James Phillips
◆ The Oba's generals
◆ Ralph Locke
◆ Rear Admiral Rawson
◆ The politicians in London

SOURCE 5 West Africa and Benin *c.* 1896.

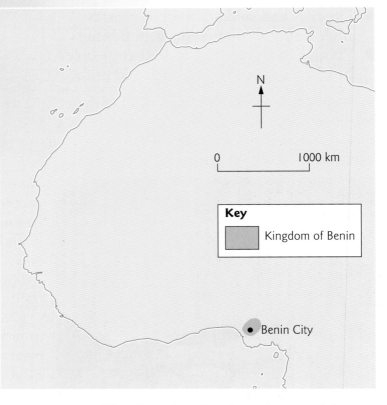

Key
▨ Kingdom of Benin

● Benin City

By the 1890s almost all of Africa was controlled by European nations. Along the West African coast, however, one kingdom still insisted on running its own affairs: the kingdom of Benin. In 1892 a British official, Captain Gallwey, travelled from the coast, where most white people were still based, to visit Benin City. He met the Oba (king) of Benin and agreed a treaty. The treaty was written in English and African translators tried to translate the words of the treaty for the Oba, who thought that he was just making a general agreement to trade with the British. In fact the words of the treaty more or less handed control of Benin over to the British.

At first all seemed to go well. The trade in spices and palm oils continued successfully and the British let the Oba rule as he liked. But by 1895 there were problems. The Oba heard how the British had used force to crush nearby African kingdoms and he was angry. He closed the trade routes to the coast. The British official in charge of that area, Ralph Moor, persuaded the Oba to open them again but Moor also sent messages to the politicians in London. He asked them to let him send troops into Benin City, to take full control of the kingdom. The politicians ordered him not to attack because they did not want Britain to be drawn into a war which would be very expensive. Moor must have been angry with this decision: he had used violence to get his way with other African chiefs and believed that it was what they understood best.

A year later Ralph Moor went on leave (holiday) and Captain James Phillips, a newly arrived official, took over. Phillips heard that British traders were angry that profits from Benin had been lower than expected. He wrote to the politicians in London and told them:

SOURCE 6

... I am certain that there is only one remedy: that is to depose the king of Benin. I am convinced that peaceful measures are now quite useless and that the time has come to move the obstruction. I do not expect any serious resistance from the people of the country, but to avoid any danger I wish to take with me sufficient armed force. I would add that I have reason to hope that sufficient riches in ivory may be found in the king's house to pay for the cost of this attack.

Without waiting for a reply to this letter, Phillips sent a message to the Oba telling him that he would be coming to see him in Benin City very soon.

However, the Oba sent messengers back to Phillips to say that he could not receive a visit for at least two months. They explained that the Oba was taking part in a ritual where his body had to be cut and scarred to please the gods and to bring blessings on the land. It would be an insult for foreigners to see him during this time.

Phillips showed no sympathy. He replied telling the Oba that he was far too busy to delay the visit and was coming anyway.

Phillips set off for Benin City early in January 1897. He took with him eight British officials and traders, with their servants. No soldiers accompanied the group.

On the way to Benin City three messengers from the Oba came to meet them. Once again they asked Phillips to turn back or to delay his visit for two days. Phillips refused and his group pushed on towards Benin City. But they never arrived.

On 4 January Phillips and his group reached a narrow forest path. Lying in wait were some of the Oba's generals. They had decided that their master was not being firm enough with the British. Without his knowledge, they had planned to kill Phillips and his party. As the group passed by they leaped upon them with spears and daggers.

Of the nine British men who set out, only two survived and struggled back to the coast. One of them later wrote a book about the ambush and called it *The Benin Massacre*. The name stuck. The other survivor, Ralph Locke, will reappear later in our story.

As soon as news of the ambush in Benin reached London, the politicians decided to punish the Oba. They sent a fleet of ships and marines to Africa under Rear Admiral Rawson, which arrived off the coast of Benin on 4 February. Rawson quickly gathered the various traders of the area, including African chiefs whose people acted as middle-men in the trade between Benin City and the coast. Rawson told the group that 'the Oba was to be no more, his town taken and his priests, if possible, killed, the Juju houses burned and the Benin Juju for ever broken . . .'.

'Juju' meant the religion of the people of Benin. The British had always deeply disliked it. To their European minds it was full of susperstition, magic and witchcraft. For years the British had chosen to ignore these beliefs, but now they intended to crush them for ever. Perhaps it was the ambush and murder of Captain Phillips that made the British take action. Or it may have been that news was reaching the coast of something even more dreadful that was taking place across Benin: human sacrifice on a massive scale.

In the weeks following the ambush of Captain Phillips, the Oba had guessed that the British would use force to try to end his power. He consulted his SOOTHSAYERS and prayed to the spirits asking how he could save his kingdom. He decided to use human sacrifice. This had been part of Benin's religion for hundreds of years, but in this time of deep crisis the Oba did not just sacrifice one or two humans, but hundreds. When Rawson's troops eventually marched towards Benin City they found hundreds of human corpses at shrines along their path. All this is described in a book written by R.H. Bacon. He called the book *Benin – City of Blood*. More bloodshed was to follow.

Rawson reached Benin City on 18 February 1897. The bows and arrows and the old guns of the Africans were no match for the modern guns, rifles and rocket tubes used by the British. By the end of that same day, Rawson had taken the city. The British set about demolishing or burning outlying huts as they closed in on the royal palace where the Oba lived. Finally the palace and the Oba himself were captured. Within days the palace was burned to the ground. The British claimed that this was an accident but no one can be sure.

The Oba was tried by British law and was banished from Benin for ever. As he was led away to be held captive for the rest of his life, the Oba could see British officers raiding his royal palace. He could only watch as white men carried off the treasures of the Obas of Benin and their mighty empire whose power no one had ever dared challenge. Those days had gone for ever and Benin was now part of a new empire – the British Empire.

Among the British officers claiming treasures from the Oba's palace that day was Ralph Locke, one of the two survivors of the so-called 'Benin massacre'. In his arms he carried a large bronze head. Once this head had been a symbol of the god-given power of the Oba; now it was a sign of the collapse of that power and of the strange period of history that we call the 'Scramble for Africa'.

Ralph Locke took the bronze head back to Britain. Eventually he passed it on to the Royal Albert Museum in Exeter. It now sits in a glass case staring out at visitors who often know little or nothing of how it came to be there and who may pass it by without thinking of what it tells us about the impact of empire.

DISCUSS

1 Which of the characters from the activity on page 78 would you most blame for the destruction of Benin City?
2 Is it fair for us to blame people for things that happened in the past? Explain your reasons.

◆ *So . . . whose head is it?*

The bronze head of Benin has been in the museum in Exeter for over 100 years now. For much of that time Benin remained within the British Empire. It is now part of the republic of Nigeria. There is a new Oba of Benin who is descended from the man who was DEPOSED in 1897. He is one of the rulers of Nigeria. He has been trying to reclaim for the people of Benin the treasures that were taken to Britain in 1897. He has been helped by Bernie Grant, a British Member of Parliament, whose ancestors came originally from Benin. Before Bernie Grant died in 2000 he wrote to every British museum that holds any objects taken from Benin in 1897. He tried to persuade each museum to return the objects to the Oba.

SOURCE 7 Bernie Grant MP.

ACTIVITY

Here are some extracts from Bernie Grant's letter to the museums. They have been mixed up with some extracts from replies he received from the museum curators.

◆ Which statements are Bernie Grant's and how can you tell?
◆ Which statements are the museum curators' and how can you tell?

> The Benin religious and cultural objects were looted in February 1897 from Benin City.

> The objects can also inform UK museum visitors about the history of the British Empire.

> Museums in Nigeria, including the one in Benin itself, already have an excellent range of ivory, carvings and bronze heads.

> Museums have a responsibility to preserve the past so that people can enjoy it and learn from it.

> The destruction of the history of the Benin people was an act of appalling racism, which must be put right. The taking of the objects from Benin is one of the most distasteful and abiding injustices arising out of the European colonisation of Africa.

> The objects introduce millions of UK museum visitors to the remarkable culture and religious beliefs of Benin.

> The British deposed the Oba of Benin in 1897 because he insisted on keeping the independence of his kingdom.

> The British took these objects as part of a battle for trade in Europe's carve up of Africa.

> If the objects are returned to the Oba and not to a Nigerian museum, they may not be seen by the public.

FINAL ACTIVITY

Who should have the head of Benin?

The Royal Albert Museum in Exeter has to decide whether the museum's bronze head should be returned to the Oba in Nigeria. Imagine that it wants to gather the views of people who visit the museum and that it has decided to set up a display or a PowerPoint presentation to explain the issues to the visitors and to seek their views.

Write five sections that will go in the display.

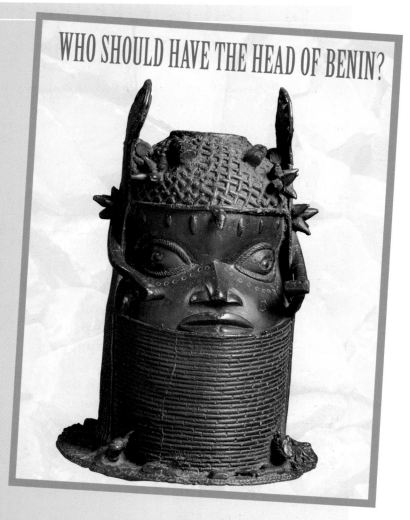

WHO SHOULD HAVE THE HEAD OF BENIN?

◆ In section A – **The background** – explain to the visitors what we mean by the 'Scramble for Africa', e.g. what happened, when it happened and why it happened. Keep it short and accurate and make it interesting (you know how people hate to read long notices in museums!). You could base this on the summary you did on page 77.

◆ In section B – **The head** – tell the story of how Ralph Locke came to own the head. Once again, keep it short, accurate and interesting. You will find what you need on pages 78–81.

◆ In section C – **Keep it?** – make a list of reasons why the museum should KEEP the head. (Include ideas even if you do not agree with them yourself.)

◆ In section D – **Return it?** – make a list of reasons why the museum should RETURN the head to the Oba. (Again, include ideas even if you do not agree with them yourself.) For both C and D you will find reasons on page 82 – but include others that you can think of as well.

◆ In Section E, your final panel or slide should just say **Visitors – what do you think?** Should the museum keep the head or return it, and why?'

Now that you have studied the story behind the Benin head and have prepared your presentation, you should be able to make up your own mind: who do *you* think should have the head of Benin?

8

IMAGES OF EMPIRE: HOW WAS THE BRITISH EMPIRE PORTRAYED?

Tackle the picture challenges to work out what children were expected to think of the British Empire

In 1897 Britain imported more bottles of champagne than ever before. The British people were celebrating Queen Victoria's 60 years on the throne. No British monarch had ever ruled for so long and a new name had to be invented for the celebration – it was called the Diamond Jubilee. At the centre of the festivities was a celebration of the Queen's Empire. During the 60 years of Queen Victoria's reign the British Empire had grown by more than ten times. The Empire now covered nearly a fifth of the Earth's surface and included a quarter of its population. In 1897 the British Empire was simply the largest empire the world had ever known.

On the morning of 22 June 1897 Queen Victoria went to the telegraph room in Buckingham Palace. She pressed an electric button and, within seconds, her Diamond Jubilee message was on its way to the far corners of her empire. The message said simply, 'From my heart I thank my beloved people. May God bless them.'

Later that day the Queen rode in a carriage through the streets of London to St Paul's Cathedral for a service of thanksgiving. The procession included 50,000 British and Empire soldiers from all over the world. Source 1 shows part of the procession with Australia's New South Wales Lancers proudly parading to St Paul's.

SOURCE 1   A photograph of Queen Victoria's Diamond Jubilee procession, 1897.

SOURCE 2 Poster advertising the Jubilee celebrations in Cannington, Somerset.

CANNINGTON.

DIAMOND JUBILEE CELEBRATION

JUNE 22nd, 1897.

A DINNER

Will be given to the WORKING MEN of Cannington, with their WIVES and FAMILIES, above the age of 15 Years, between the hours of 12 and 2, at the "Anchor" Inn.

Application for **Dinner Tickets** to be made to Mr. Martin not later than June 11th.

A PROCESSION

Will be formed at the "Anchor" headed by the

STOGURSEY BRASS BAND,

AT 2-30 P.M., TO MARCH TO THE PARK.

ATHLETIC SPORTS

Confined to the Parishioners of Cannington,

WILL BE HELD IN THE PARK, and a

TEA FOR THE SCHOOL CHILDREN.

DANCING FROM 7 TO 9.

FIREWORKS AT 9.   BONFIRE AT 10.

N.B.--The Friendly Societies have consented to join the Procession.

GOD SAVE THE QUEEN !!

The Jubilee was also celebrated in towns and villages all over Britain. For several days in June 1897 there were parades, speeches, religious services, balls, street parties and concerts. The poster in Source 2 is advertising the festivities at Cannington in Somerset.

However, not everyone in Britain at the end of the nineteenth century was a strong supporter of the Empire. Some people thought that the whole idea of empire was wrong. Others were ignorant about how the Empire worked. At the turn of the century the imperialists (supporters of empire) thought that it was important to make British citizens, especially children and young people, feel proud of their country and empire. Some of the images you will see in this chapter were designed to do just this. They are therefore useful for finding out what the imperialists wanted the younger generation to think about the Empire.

YOUR ENQUIRY

Queen Victoria's Diamond Jubilee was one way in which British citizens were made to feel proud. But there were many other ways that the British Empire could be promoted. In this enquiry you will find out about the different images of empire which were presented to children and young people. You will have to think hard about the messages behind these images if you want to do well in the picture challenges. Let's begin with the images of the Empire which children would have seen in school.

◆ The Empire in school

The most obvious way to encourage children to value the Empire was through their schools. From 1902 many schools celebrated Empire Day on 24 May each year. The idea was for pupils and teachers to spend a day concentrating on the glories of the British Empire. Pupils learned facts about the Empire and sang PATRIOTIC songs. In some schools children took the parts of heroes from the Empire, such as Robert Clive or James Wolfe. In other schools pupils dressed up to represent people from different colonies, each paying their respects to their 'mother', Britannia (who was often the tallest girl in the school). In these ways schoolchildren created their own images of the British Empire.

SOURCE 3   A photograph of a school's Empire Day celebrations in 1923.

PICTURE CHALLENGE

Look at Source 3.

1 How are the children dressed?
2 What are the children doing?
3 What messages about the British Empire were reinforced on Empire Day?

Not everyone in Britain agreed with Empire Day. Some people thought that children were being brainwashed into supporting the British Empire. However, most schools joined in, perhaps because the afternoon was a holiday!

Schoolchildren also learned about the Empire from maps in their textbooks and on their classroom wall. This map of the world was made in 1886. Britain's territories are coloured pink. The map exaggerates the size of Britain compared to other countries. If you look carefully at the map you will also find lots of other messages about the British Empire.

SOURCE 4 A map of the British Empire in 1886.

PICTURE CHALLENGE 2

Look at Source 4.

1 Find out the meanings of the words at the top of the map. What do these words tell us about British attitudes towards the Empire?

2 At the sides and bottom of the map are people and symbols from Britain's colonies. Identify as many of these as you can. What do the symbols suggest about British attitudes towards the colonies?

3 How does the map show that Britain gained her empire through navy and sea power?

4 Write a short paragraph to sum up the message behind the map.

◆ The Empire in fiction

A hundred years ago children and young people did not watch television, surf the internet or play computer games; they read magazines, comics and novels. Many of these publications featured stories set overseas in the British colonies. Children loved these exciting adventures that took place in strange lands. However, many of the stories portrayed the British as heroes, while the native people appeared as either servants or savages. You can see some of these images in Sources 5–7.

SOURCE 5 The front cover of a children's storybook from 1926.

SOURCE 6 The front cover of a boys' magazine from 1924.

SOURCE 7 An illustration from a story in a magazine, 1917.

PICTURE CHALLENGE 3

Look at Sources 5–7.

1 How did these images try to glorify Britain, or British people?
2 How did these images suggest that the native people were inferior to the British?
3 Which of these images would be considered most offensive today?

◆ *The Empire in advertising*

Another way in which children were shown images of the Empire was in advertisements. At the beginning of the twentieth century many companies used the Empire to boost sales of their products. The examples in Sources 8–10 show some of the ways the Empire was used in advertising.

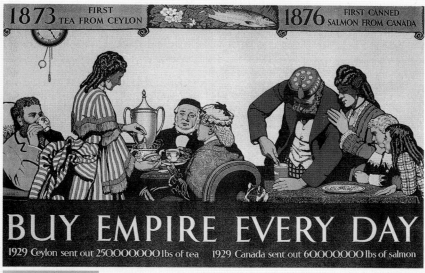

SOURCE 8

SOURCE 9

SOURCE 10

PICTURE CHALLENGE 4

For each advertisement in Sources 8–10:

1 work out what product was being advertised
2 describe the images of empire contained in the advertisement
3 explain why you think the advertisers used these images of empire.

◆ *The Empire and Scouting*

SOURCE 11 A photograph of Lieutenant General Robert Baden-Powell, 1907.

Look at Source 11. In 1907 this man founded the Boy Scout movement. He is Lieutenant General Robert Baden-Powell. Baden-Powell was a soldier in the British army who became a national hero during Britain's war against the Boers in South Africa. He wanted Britain's boys to grow up into strong and active citizens who would be able to defend the British Empire. Scouts had to follow the Scout Law at all times. This meant that they had to be:

◆ trustworthy
◆ loyal to their king and country
◆ helpful to others
◆ obedient to their parents or Scout leader
◆ cheerful at all times!

In the years after 1907 tens of thousands of boys joined the Scouts. In 1910 the Girl Guide movement was formed in order to give girls similar experiences. Scouting soon spread across the British Empire.

SOURCE 12 A photograph showing Robert Baden-Powell with Scouts from different parts of the Empire at the Imperial Jamboree, London, 1924.

Robert Baden-Powell's book, *Scouting for Boys*, became a huge best-seller after its publication in 1908. The book contained details of the Scout Law as well as practical advice and stories of adventure at home and abroad.

SOURCE 13 A Scouting Association publicity photograph, 1910.

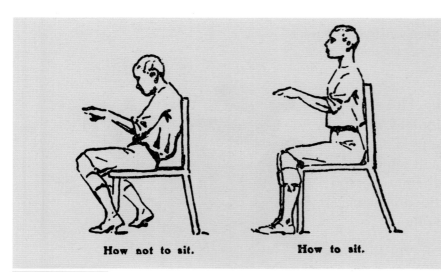

How not to sit.　　How to sit.

SOURCE 14 An illustration from *Scouting for Boys*, 1908.

PICTURE CHALLENGE 5

Source 12

1 Do you think this picture was an official or an unofficial photograph?
2 What is the message of the photograph?

Source 13

3 Why do you think this picture might persuade boys to join the Scouts?

Source 14

4 What does this picture tell us about Baden-Powell's attitudes?

◆ *Lantern slides of the Empire*

At the end of the nineteenth century lantern slide shows were a popular form of entertainment. During the winter months, adults and children would crowd into village halls, schools, theatres and church rooms to see photographs or pictures projected onto large screens. In 1907 the Colonial Office in London came up with a special scheme to teach children about the British Empire. They planned a series of lantern slide shows about life in different parts of the Empire. Once again, the aim was to make children feel proud to be citizens of the British Empire.

The Colonial Office appointed an official photographer, Hugh Fisher. Fisher was paid to travel around the British Empire for three years, taking thousands of photographs for the lantern slide shows. Before Fisher left Britain in October 1907, the Colonial Office instructed him to take photographs of . . .

> . . . the native characteristics of the country and the super-added characteristics due to British rule.

DISCUSS

1 What do you think the Colonial Office's instruction meant?
2 Why do you think the Colonial Office gave this instruction?

Hugh Fisher first travelled to India. He sent back hundreds of pictures and the Colonial Office selected the ones which would be used. On the following pages you will find a small sample of Fisher's photographs. Of course, the photographs give us a very selective and one-sided view of British India. They represent the official, Colonial Office, view. However, they are very useful for finding out the way in which the Empire was portrayed to British children.

SOURCE 15 St Mary's Church in Madras.

SOURCE 17 Snake charmers at Benares.

SOURCE 18 A view of the Lansdowne Bridge over the river Indus.

SOURCE 19 A burning ghat (cremation) at Benares.

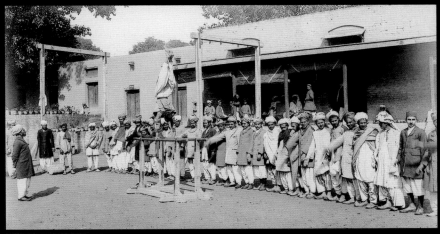

SOURCE 20 A gymnastics class at the Government High School, Peshwar.

YOUR FINAL PICTURE CHALLENGE

Imagine that you are an official at the Colonial Office in 1907. You can select three of Hugh Fisher's photographs to include in one of the lantern slide shows about British India.

Look again at the instructions that the Colonial Office gave to Fisher (page 92). Now select your three photographs from pages 93–95. Write a short report explaining what message you hope each of the photographs will convey about British India.

LAND OF HOPE AND GLORY
Play Mix and Match to summarise another 120 years of empire

In 1901 Queen Victoria died. Her long reign saw the British Empire – and British pride – grow enormously. In that same year the new king, Edward VII, heard a piece of music that seemed to capture this mood. It was by the English composer Edward Elgar, and was called Pomp and Circumstance. King Edward suggested that words be written to accompany the melody. The work was complete by 1902, and in 1911 it was sung at the coronation of King George V. Since then, British audiences have sung the song at events such as football matches, and at the last night of the Proms. Here is the famous chorus:

Land of Hope and Glory, Mother of the Free,
How shall we extol thee, who are born of thee?
Wider still and wider shall thy bounds be set;
God, who made thee mighty, make thee mightier yet.
God, who made thee mighty, make thee mightier yet.

Chapters 5 to 8 of this book have shown how Britain's empire grew 'Wider still and wider' from the start of the nineteenth century. You can see the change by comparing the map below with the one on page 48. In both maps, the red areas represent the British Empire.

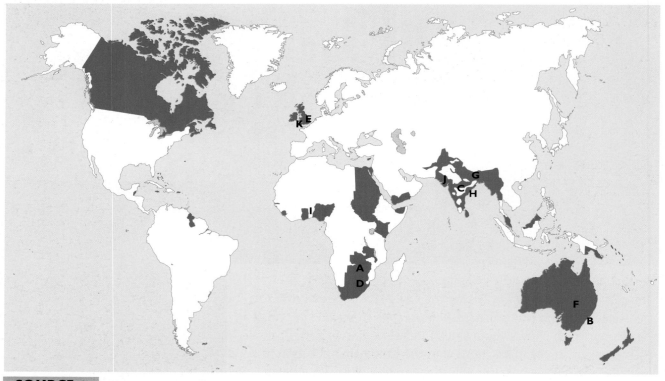

SOURCE 1 The British Empire in 1914.

ACTIVITY A

All these people were involved in the story of the British Empire between 1783 and 1911. Match each one with the correct letter on the map.

◆ **Captain Arthur Phillip** set up Britain's first convict settlement in Sydney, Australia in 1788 (see pages 50–56).

◆ **William Carey** was a missionary who spread Christianity to India (1797). He also worked with **Rammohan Roy**, a Hindu, to end the Indian custom of widow burning (see pages 64–65).

◆ **Aborigines** in Australia and Maoris in New Zealand lost their land to British cattle and sheep farms after 1800 (see pages 57–59).

◆ **Miss Williams** was the child of a British soldier. She died at Cawnpore in 1857 when thousands of Indians revolted against the way the British ruled their land (see pages 68–70).

◆ **Lord Mayo** and 5000 officials ruled India on behalf of Queen Victoria (1872). He called the Indians 'an inferior race' (see page 71).

◆ **David Livingstone** was the Scottish missionary who hoped to spread Christianity and western civilization in Africa (1875), and opened the way for the 'Scramble for Africa' (see pages 76–77).

◆ **Dadabhai Naoriji** was an Indian who became a Member of Parliament in London in 1892. He complained that British rules of trading made Britain rich and kept India poor (see pages 72–73).

◆ **The Oba of Benin** lost his African kingdom and his treasures when British soldiers conquered his lands in 1897 (see pages 78–82).

◆ **Lord Baden Powell** became a hero when he fought as a soldier in the Boer War in South Africa (1899–1902) (see pages 90–91).

◆ **Hugh Fisher** took photographs (1907) of the Empire, including pictures of railways, hospitals and schools being built, English being taught, and British sports being played (see pages 92–95).

SOURCE 2 Statue of Queen Victoria in city of Victoria, Canada

ACTIVITY B

Link each of these statements to one or more of the developments listed above.
By 1911 ...

◆ British museums were full of objects from across the Empire
◆ Cricket and rugby were popular sports around the Empire
◆ New Zealand shipped frozen lamb to Britain
◆ Some native customs disappeared for ever as the Empire grew
◆ Christianity was stronger in parts of Africa than in parts of Britain
◆ Some Britons looked down on the native peoples of the Empire
◆ British industries and cities grew rich by trading with the colonies
◆ Boy Scouts and Girl Guides learned to be loyal and helpful
◆ The British put up statues and monuments for Empire builders
◆ British charities gave to hospitals and schools around the Empire
◆ British schools taught children to be proud of the Empire

DISCUSS

Do any of these developments still affect life in Britain today?

9

IRELAND: WHY DO PEOPLE TELL DIFFERENT STORIES ABOUT IRELAND AND THE BRITISH EMPIRE?

Get ready to make your voice heard on a radio phone-in

◆ Fighting for the British Empire

When King George V declared war on Germany in August 1914 he did so, not only for Britain, but for all 450 million people in the British Empire.

The biggest army under British orders in 1914 was the Indian Army, led by British officers, with 155,000 men, mostly Indians and including many Sikhs. They were soon holding large sections of the British line on the Western Front.

Many Irishmen also answered the imperial call to arms. Over 200,000 fought in the British Army in the First World War, of whom 30,000 died. They were encouraged by recruiting posters like the one in source 2. Obviously many Irishmen were ready to swear allegiance to the king, and fight for Britain and the British Empire.

SOURCE 1 Indian soldiers fighting in the First World War.

◆ Fighting against Britain

However, not everyone in the British Empire was ready to fight for Britain.

On Easter Saturday 1916, a group of armed Irish men and women took control of fourteen buildings – including the central Post Office – in Ireland's capital city, Dublin. The rebels' leader, Patrick Pearse, proclaimed an independent Irish Republic, free from British rule.

SOURCE 2 British army recruitment poster used in Ireland in the First World War.

SOURCE 3 The General Post Office lies in ruins after the Easter Uprising of 1916.

The Irish rebels numbered only 1200. They had rifles but no artillery. Most of the British Army was fighting in France, but the government in London rapidly sent 20,000 men, a gunboat, and heavy artillery to Dublin. The rebels thought that the British would not use heavy guns on the occupied buildings, because many of them were British-owned. In fact the British military commanders had no such reservations, and were under orders to crush the rebellion as soon as possible. Within a few days large areas of central Dublin lay in ruins. Hopelessly outnumbered and with no sign of popular support, the rebels surrendered the following Saturday.

One island, two different attitudes: some Irishmen were prepared to die fighting for King and Empire in France; other Irishmen were prepared to die fighting against King and Empire in Dublin. How did this happen?

YOUR ENQUIRY

One of the biggest factors in deciding who you are is your heritage, your history. But does history stay the same when different people look at the same events from different standpoints?

Ireland was part of the British Empire for centuries, but British rule caused divisions in Ireland that have lasted to the present day. In this enquiry you will find out about some key events in Irish history and think about what each side would say about them. At the end you will get ready to have your say on an Irish radio phone-in programme about history.

My name is Ian. I am a Unionist.
I feel I belong to Britain and want Ireland to stay part of the United Kingdom.

My grandfather fought for Britain at the Battle of the Somme.
I think …
I think the Easter Rising was …

My name is Patrick. I am a Nationalist.
I feel Ireland should be an independent country ruling itself, not by Britain.

My gradfather took part in the Easter Rising. I think it was …
I think those Irish people who fought in the British army were …

Ian

Patrick

ACTIVITY

Copy the words from the speech bubbles. Fill in the gaps with what you think Ian and Patrick would say.

◆ Two histories

The kings of England had called themselves kings of Ireland since 1155, but the Irish had always resisted English conquest. They had their own language, laws, music, culture, and religion. When England turned Protestant in the sixteenth century, Ireland did not. This changed the situation. England's Roman Catholic enemies, like Spain, could use Ireland as a safe base from which to attack England, only a few miles away across the Irish Sea. Large English armies were sent to keep Ireland's Catholics under control.

English settlement: the 'plantations'

In 1601 the English defeated the Irish in north-east Ireland – the area called Ulster. They came up with a plan to end the danger posed by Ireland. The English government took over Ulster and offered it to Protestant English or Scottish settlers. About ten settler families were 'planted' on every 1000 acres. Planned, fortified villages were built all over Ulster, like Bellaghy, planted in 1621. In total, 100,000 Protestant settlers came to live in Ulster.

In 1603 Roman Catholics owned 90 per cent of the land in Ireland; by 1641 they owned only 59 per cent.

Their experiences in Ireland gave the British two models they could apply later as the Empire grew:

1 **Plantations.** The farms set up in the Caribbean – using slaves to grow special crops such as sugar to sell to Britain – were also called 'PLANTATIONS'.
2 **Colonies.** The sequence of conquest, taking over the land, and then offering it to British settlers, was used in many parts of the Empire to create colonies.

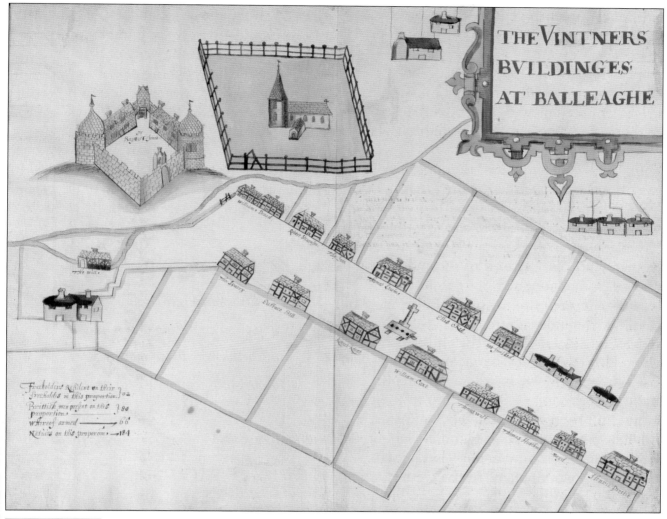

SOURCE 4   A contemporary map of Bellaghy plantation, settled by the Vintners Company, of London.

ACTIVITY

Source 4 shows a map of Bellaghy plantation, one of the new fortified villages in Ulster.
Find:

◆ The fortified house, or bawn. It was occupied by the English planter, Sir Baptist Jones, and provided refuge if settlers were attacked by the Irish.
◆ The Protestant church and churchyard.
◆ The market cross, where markets were held. Nearby are the stocks for punishing law-breakers – using English laws.
◆ Planters' houses. Solid, quite large, timber-framed, two-storey dwellings with dormer windows for attic rooms, and chimneys for the fireplaces.
◆ The smaller, single-storey houses of the Irish. They now worked as labourers for the English and Scottish planters.

◆ *A violent history*

In the seventeenth century there was violence between Irish and British on both sides.

The Irish in Ulster rose up in rebellion in 1641, mainly because of the plantations. Protestant settlers were killed, perhaps 2000 of them, and many of the planted towns burned.

In 1649, fresh from his triumphs in battle over the Royalist armies in the English Civil War, Oliver Cromwell arrived in Ireland with an army. He besieged the town of Drogheda and called on the Royalist, mainly Roman Catholic garrison to surrender. They refused, so he launched his attack. His soldiers captured the town and killed most of the 2000 defenders. Some townspeople took refuge in the church, but they all perished when Cromwell had it set ablaze.

Cromwell followed up his campaign in Ireland by driving 40,000 Irish from their farms, and then giving the land to his ex-soldiers. The Irish became landless labourers, working for their new English landlords. Some fled to Connaught in the west of Ireland, where the soil was poor, and making a living was difficult. By 1665, only 22 per cent of land in Ireland was owned by Catholics.

By the 1690s, British Protestant control was even stronger. Roman Catholics were not allowed to vote, attend university, run schools, or even own a horse worth more than £5. Ireland was inhabited by a minority of Protestant, English-speaking landowners who dominated the majority of Roman Catholic, Gaelic-speaking peasants.

The memory of Cromwell is still powerful in Ireland even 300 years later. The Nationalist and Unionist communities remember him in different ways. He is a hate figure to the Nationalists, as demonstrated in the lyrics of the song *Young Ned of the Hill*, by The Pogues, written as recently as 1989:

> *A curse upon you Oliver Cromwell*
>
> *You who raped our Motherland*
>
> *I hope you're rotting down in hell*
>
> *For the horrors that you sent*
>
> *To our misfortunate forefathers*
>
> *Whom you robbed of their birthright*
>
> *'To hell or Connaught' may you burn in hell tonight.*

However, to Unionists he is hero, whose picture can be seen on street mural paintings in Protestant areas like the one shown in Source 5.

SOURCE 5 A recent wall painting of Oliver Cromwell in a protestant area of Northern Ireland

ACTIVITY

You met Ian (the Unionist) and Patrick (the Nationalist) on page 99. Here they are again.

Which event would Ian choose to remember from these pages?

Which event would Patrick choose?

Write in Ian and Patrick's speech bubbles what each one would say about the event he has chosen.

Write what Ian and Patrick would say about the other's choice.

◆ *The Irish Famine*

Ireland in the nineteenth century was as much a part of Britain as England was. MPs were elected from Irish constituencies to the British Parliament in London; English landowners built large country houses on their Irish estates. Most Irish were farmers, some with good-sized farms, but many had very little land.

The population of Ireland rose quickly, from 5.2 million in 1801, to 8.2 million in 1841. More people living on the same amount of land meant that families had to survive on less, sometimes only a quarter of an acre. How could a family be fed from a quarter of an acre?

There is a one-word answer to this question: **potatoes**. Potatoes grow well in Ireland's climate. One acre of land can produce six to eight tons of potatoes a year. They were grown in 'lazy beds', so-called because they required little work. Each year, soil was turned on top of last year's remains, and seeds were planted. Many poor Irish families ate nothing but potatoes and buttermilk, flavoured with a little bacon, or cabbage.

Then disaster! In 1845 potato blight reached Ireland. The potato crops in the fields were reduced to stinking, inedible rot. How could poor people survive? That year they sold everything they had to buy food. But the blight returned in 1846 and again in 1847. Most people had nothing left to sell, and had eaten their seed potatoes. They began to starve to death in the streets and in their homes. Weakened by hunger, many died of disease, such as typhus and cholera. When they became too penniless to pay their rent, landlords evicted them from their homes. Many dug holes in the ground to live in. Some ate the bodies of the recently died.

SOURCE 6   A starving Irish family drawn in 1900.

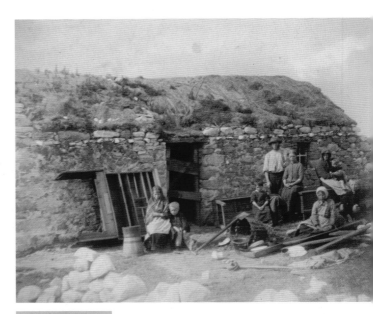

SOURCE 7   A family being evicted from their home in the 1880s, which is to be pulled down to prevent them moving back.

Who tried to help?

There was a good deal of anti-Irish racism in England at that time; the Irish were portrayed as lazy, drunken, violent layabouts. The British government believed that people should not be given handouts of food: they must buy it. Starving people were made to work – building roads, for example – to earn money, even though many were weakened by hunger.

Charities stepped in. The Quakers were particularly active, setting up soup kitchens in the worst affected areas. In many towns in western Ireland they were feeding three-quarters of the population each day.

SOURCE 8 Modern statues of starving Irish emigrants, Dublin.

What were the results of the Famine?

◆ One million people died.
◆ Another million emigrated. Some came to Britain. Many more went to the USA and parts of the British Empire, such as Australia and Canada. Ireland became an empty land.
◆ Long-lasting bitterness. Irish emigrants did not want to leave their homes, but despaired of making a living in Ireland. There was also a legacy of bitterness towards the British government, because of its failure to help during the FAMINE.

ACTIVITY

1 'Nature causes crop failures; human beings cause famines.' Use what you have found out about the Irish Famine to discuss what this means.
2 Which people would Patrick blame for the Famine? Write your answer in Patrick's speech bubble, and explain his choice.
3 Do the same for Ian.
4 Copy the speech bubbles and write in them who Ian and Patrick would praise for their behaviour during the Famine, and why.
5 What other factors, apart from people, were to blame for the million deaths in the Irish Famine?

◆ What happened after the Easter Rising?

It was memories of the Famine and anger at England's continual interference in Irish history that drove Patrick Pearse and his friends to launch their Easter Rising in 1916. At first few Irish people supported the rebels. Subsequent events changed everyone's views. The British government gave the rebels a brief trial and then, one by one, they were executed by firing squad. One man, James Connolly, dying of his wounds, was propped up in a chair and shot. Hundreds of Nationalists who had not taken part in the Easter Rising were arrested and imprisoned.

This brutal response swung Irish opinion in favour of independence. In the 1918 elections, many seats all over Ireland (except in Ulster) were won by candidates who wanted Ireland to be a free, independent, republic, separate from the British Empire. The elected MPs refused to go to London to sit in the British Parliament and formed their own government in Dublin.

Irish Republicans attacked representatives of British rule. By 1920, 55 policemen had been killed and sixteen police barracks burnt down. Once again the British government's reaction made things worse. 8000 men were recruited, armed, and sent to Ireland. They became known as the Black and Tans because of the mixture of police (black) and army (tan) uniforms they wore. Many had been soldiers in the First World War. They were experienced killers, but not trained in police work which involves working within the law.

Some idea of their attitude is demonstrated in these orders issued by a Black and Tan officer, Lieutenant Colonel Smyth, in June 1920:

Should the order ('Hands Up') not be immediately obeyed, shoot and shoot with effect. If the persons approaching (a patrol) carry their hands in their pockets, or are in any way suspicious-looking, shoot them down. You may make mistakes occasionally and innocent persons may be shot, but that cannot be helped, and you are bound to get the right parties some time.

This policy was secretly agreed to by the British government.

A cycle of retaliation and death began. In November 1920 the Irish Republicans shot fourteen government detectives they had caught. In retaliation, the Black and Tans sent armoured cars into the football stadium at Croke Park, in Dublin, and shot into the crowd, killing twelve people. In retaliation eighteen Black and Tans were ambushed and killed in County Cork. In retaliation the Black and Tans burnt down the centre of Cork city.

SOURCE 9 Two armed Black and Tans, with a policeman and a soldier.

Partition, 1921

By 1921, 1300 people had been killed, including 550 members of the British forces. It was clear that as the death toll mounted, neither side was winning. The British government was not prepared to give Ireland complete independence, or to abandon Ulster, where the Protestant and Unionist descendants of the Plantations and Cromwell's land changes were in the majority. In the end a deal was reached and a treaty signed.

As the map shows, Ireland was 'partitioned' – divided. The six counties of Ulster remained part of the UK. The rest of Ireland became the Irish Free State.

1921 saw independence for **part** of Ireland. This is a key date in the story of the break-up of the British Empire, marking the first time a former colony had successfully fought for its independence, and won.

The 1921 Treaty is also an example of PARTITION – trying to make peace by separating different people – used in the twentieth century. You will find other examples in Chapter 11.

SOURCE 10 Map of Ireland, showing partition between the Republic of Ireland and Northern Ireland, part of the UK.

ACTIVITY

HISTORY: Study it, or forget it?
In 2007 an Irish Senator, David Norris, was interviewed on Irish radio. He was asked what he would like to change about Ireland. Part of his reply is given below.

'I would change our continuing wish to live in the past and re-fight old battles.' *Senator David Norris*

What do you think Ian and Patrick would say if they phoned in to the radio station to reply to Senator Norris?
Look back over the work you have done and use some of the speech bubbles you have prepared for Ian and Patrick to help you.
Is it ever possible to forget the past?
Is it fair to say that Patrick and Ian gained their view of the past by 'studying' history?
Is it ever likely that we can solve problems in places like Ireland without studying the historical roots of the issues?
Finally, what do you, as a young person in the twenty-first century think about what Senator Norris said?

SOURCE 11 Senator David Norris.

10

HIGH HOPES: WHAT HELPED AND HINDERED GERTRUDE'S DREAMS FOR THE ARABS?

Improve a hopeless internet encyclopaedia

After the First World War, Britain ruled large parts of the Middle East. This photograph was taken in 1921 when British politicians and advisers met at Cairo to discuss their plans for the region.

On the left is Winston Churchill, Britain's minister for the colonies. The small figure near the centre is T.E. Lawrence. You may have seen the film *Lawrence of Arabia*, in which he wears traditional Arab robes (like the guide, standing to the left of the picture).

Between Churchill and Lawrence sits Gertrude Bell. Like Lawrence, she loved the Arab people of the Middle East. From 1900 to 1913, she crossed their deserts and mountains, sailed their great rivers, learned their language, excavated their ancient cities, and formed deep friendships with their leaders.

A thousand years ago, the Middle East had been the centre of a great Islamic empire whose wealth, art and science outshone anything in Europe. Gertrude dreamed of restoring a great Arab CIVILISATION, made up of many tribes. For years she worked to make her dream come true. But what helped her, and what hindered her? And were her high hopes fulfilled? Let's see.

SOURCE 1 British officials in Cairo 1921

SOURCE 2 Gertrude Bell (1868–1926).

◆ Britain and the Middle East

In the first three centuries of the British Empire, Britain had shown little interest in the Middle East. By 1914 this had changed. Three reasons for this change are listed below. Source 3 will help you.

SOURCE 3 Map showing the Middle East in 1914.

- ◆ The Suez Canal opened in 1869. It cut through Egypt and shortened Britain's valuable sea route to India. Britain wanted to control the area around the canal. In 1878 she took charge of the island of Cyprus, and in 1882 her troops occupied Egypt.

- ◆ In 1908 a British company struck oil in south-west Persia (modern Iran). In 1911, Britain decided to use oil to fuel her ships; now she had to protect her oil supplies in the Persian Gulf.

- ◆ In 1914 the main power in the Middle East was the Muslim Ottoman Empire, based in modern Turkey. The Turks were allies of Germany. So, when war broke out in 1914, the British and Turks fought each other in the Middle East. Britain was fighting to gain control of Turkey's lands in Syria, Palestine, Mesopotamia and the Hijaz. Most people in these lands were Arabs.

As you can see, the Middle East was a complicated area. In 1915, to help win the war against the Ottoman Empire, the British government called for help from the western world's leading expert on Arab life; her name was Gertrude Bell.

◆ *Promises, promises*

Between 1914 and 1918 soldiers from the British Empire fought in the deserts of the Middle East against the Turks. Far away from the conflict, politicians were making the big decisions about the war and what should happen afterwards. They relied on expert advisers like Gertrude Bell. Gertrude hoped she could help the politicians create a great new Arab civilisation. But the politicians often did what they wanted, no matter what she might advise.

Read about these three promises that British politicians made to different groups during the war. Think how each promise might help or hinder Gertrude's dream of a great new Arab civilisation

Promise 1: Britain's deal with the Arabs

Between 1915 and 1916, Britain's leader in Egypt, Sir Henry McMahon, had a secret correspondence with a powerful Arab leader called Hussein, the Sharif of Makah. (Hussein liked to send his secret messages in dagger hilts and the soles of shoes!)

Hussein resented Turkish rule. He told McMahon that he would help the British by organising an army of Arab tribesmen to fight the Turks, but only if Britain promised to help the Arabs to rule themselves after the war.

In October 1915 McMahon agreed to Hussein's demands. However, his final agreement in 1916 was deliberately vague about the borders and government of any new Arab lands. Hussein was pleased to have done the deal and said the details could be sorted out after the war.

Gertrude Bell only became McMahon's adviser just after the main agreement was reached. Although she wanted the Arabs to win their freedom, she was worried. She was sure that Hussein expected to become the leader of a single Arab nation stretching across the Middle East – but she guessed that McMahon had no intention of letting this happen. The British would want to keep control over the areas near Suez and near their oilfields.

Despite her concerns, Gertrude said nothing to upset the deal. In June 1916, Arab warriors, led by Hussein's son Feisal, joined the British in their desert war against the Turks.

SOURCE 4   Sharif Hussein.

SOURCE 5   Arab troops ride into battle.
Courtesy of the Imperial War Museum.

Promise 2: Britain's deal with the French

Just days before the Arabs rode out to fight the Turks in 1916, the British made another deal. The Arabs knew nothing about it. It was known as the Sykes-Picot Agreement, named after the two officials who wrote it. If they won the war, Britain and France planned to take land for themselves in the Middle East, and to divide the rest into 'areas of influence', setting up forms of government to suit themselves.

Gertrude Bell was alarmed when she learned of this deal. Britain was ignoring her promises to Hussein by secretly planning to take control of Arab lands. But Gertrude said nothing in public.

SOURCE 6   The division of the Middle East proposed by the Sykes-Picot agreement.

Promise 3: Britain's deal with the Jews

In 70 AD the Romans had driven the Jewish people from their ancient homeland in Palestine. Since then, the Jews had spread throughout the world, and had often been persecuted, especially in Europe. By 1900 some Jews, called Zionists, were determined to return to Palestine. A scientist called Chaim Weizmann led Britain's Zionists.

In 1915 Weizmann developed a new way of mass-producing explosives for the British army. He urged a grateful British government to back the Zionist cause. The government also wanted to win support for the war from Jews in America. In November 1917 the Foreign Secretary, Arthur Balfour, made his famous Balfour Declaration in a letter to a leading British Jew.

Gertrude Bell was alarmed: 700,000 Arabs already lived in Palestine. By offering it as a homeland to Jews, Britain seemed to break its deal with Hussein, who expected the Arabs to rule the region. She feared the Arabs would no longer support Britain against Turkey. She also feared the deal would sow bitterness between Arabs and Jews, ruining the chances of a peaceful Middle East.

SOURCE 7   The Balfour Declaration

ACTIVITY

Improve this next section of the Wackypedia entry. Use pages 110–111 to help you.

In the Second World War, British politicians made several deals to help win the war against the Turkish Otterman Empire. Gertrude was sure these deals would help give power to the Arabs.

◆ *From war to peace*

In 1917 the Sykes-Picot agreement leaked to the public, just as Britain published the Balfour Declaration. Hussein was furious. He accused the British of deceiving him, but they assured Hussein that the Sykes-Picot proposals had been dropped and that allowing Jews into Palestine would not take away the rights of the Arabs who lived there. Hussein was satisfied. His Arab troops continued fighting.

The war finally ended in November 1918. The Ottoman Empire had lost control of the Middle East. But who would rule it in future? And would Britain keep any of the promises it had made to the Arabs, the French and the Jews? All this depended on the Peace Conference that began in Paris in January 1919.

In Paris the victorious nations were led by the United States, France and Britain. They decided that the defeated empires of Germany, Austria, Russia and Turkey must lose much of their land.

The politicians agreed to follow the principle of 'self-determination', giving each national group in the defeated empires the right to have its own country. This is exactly what Gertrude wanted for the Arabs.

The conference also decided that new nations in

SOURCE 8 A meeting at the Paris Peace Conference 1919.

the Middle East should be 'mandates'. This meant that they would be governed at first by more powerful nations such as Britain and France, who had to prepare them for the time when they would rule themselves. Source 9 shows the mandates covering the old Ottoman Empire.

Gertrude liked the idea of mandates as she believed the different Arabs groups would need help before they could rule themselves as modern states. But she was disappointed to learn that the Arab lands were to be split between Britain and France.

DISCUSS

Did this mandate system mean Britain was keeping the promise it made to Hussein in 1916? (See page 110).

Gertrude Bell attended the Paris peace conference as one of Britain's experts. She hoped that it would begin the re-birth of the great Arab civilization she longed to see. She faced several disappointments:

◆ The conference was dominated by big powers. Smaller groups such as the Arabs had little say in the decisions. The only Arab representative was Hussein's son Prince Feisal.
◆ The politicians knew little about the Middle East, yet they often refused to listen to advice from experts like Gertrude.
◆ The politicians invented a new organisation called the League of Nations. It would draw borders across the lands of the old empires to create new nations. However, it would take years to set up and even longer to do its work.
◆ Prince Feisal seemed to think the Palestinians were not true Arabs. To Gertrude's surprise, he reached an agreement with the Zionist leader, Weizmann, accepting Jewish migration into Palestine.
◆ Palestinians were not directly represented at the conference. With Britain in charge of the Palestinian mandate, they knew that Jewish immigration was sure to go ahead as Balfour had promised. The Palestinians had no say in the matter. They were angry that Feisal had failed to speak up for them. It looked as though Gertrude's hopes for a united Arab civilisation had been lost already!

Gertrude wrote to a friend about what was happening in Paris:

O my dear, they are making such a horrible muddle of the Near East. I confidently anticipate that it will be much worse than it was before the war … It's like a nightmare in which you foresee all the horrible things which are going to happen and can't stretch out your hand to prevent them.

Gertrude thought the main problems concerned Syria and Palestine – the Near East. She dearly hoped that she could help avoid chaos in the British mandate in Mesopotamia – now called Iraq. It would not be easy.

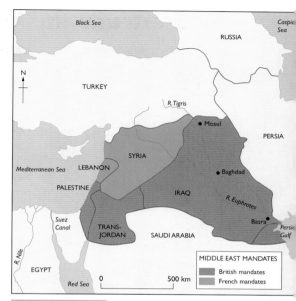

SOURCE 9   Middle East mandates.

SOURCE 10   Weizmann and Feisal after reaching their agreement on Palestine in 1919. Weizmann is wearing an Arab headdress as a sign of friendship.

ACTIVITY

Here is another Wackypedia entry about Gertrude. It claims that the Paris Conference helped the Arabs gain independence. This is too simple. Use pages 112 to 113 to show how decisions at the conference helped and hindered the Arab cause.
Add any other changes: Is it fair to say Britain won the war? When did all this happen? Was Gertrude proud?

After Britain won the war against the Ottoman Empire, Gertrude attended the Paris Peace Conference. She was proud of the way it helped the Arabs gain their independence.

◆ Gertrude the king-maker

SOURCE 11 Baghdad in 1920

In March 1917, about eighteen months before the end of the war, British and Indian troops captured Baghdad from the Turks. It was the main city of Mesopotamia – or Iraq as it is now called, after the Arabic name for the region. Within weeks Gertrude Bell moved there to advise on British rule. Gertrude was eager to press on with the work of creating her ideal Arab state in Iraq. But continued fighting in the north, delays at the Peace Conference and months of discussions in the League of Nations about the borders of Iraq, all caused difficulties. As time went by it became obvious that there were deep divisions in this newly designed nation.

- ◆ There were splits between the two main groups of Muslims – Shi'ites and Sunnis – who had been rivals for centuries.
- ◆ There were splits between the Arabs, who lived in most of Iraq, and the Kurds, who lived in the northern region of Mosul.
- ◆ The Kurds hoped that the League of Nations would grant them a country of their own. Britain wanted to keep Mosul in Iraq as they were sure it had rich oil fields.
- ◆ There were splits between educated city Muslims and the tribes of the deserts.
- ◆ There were splits between Arabs who were happy to work with the British and Arab nationalists, who wanted the British to leave straightaway so that Iraq could rule itself.

By 1920 there was a large-scale revolt in much of Iraq and the British could barely keep control. One army garrison retreated by boarding a train and lifting up rails behind them and re-laying the track at the front to carry them 60 miles to a safer base! Britain used its air power to bomb Iraqi and Kurdish towns that resisted British rule. They even used gas attacks.

Gertrude had some sympathy with the Arab nationalists and disliked the use of brute force, but she was sure that order had to be restored. In April 1920 she wrote: … *if we leave this country to go to the dogs, we shall have to reconsider our whole position in Asia. If Iraq goes, Persia goes inevitably, then India. The place which we leave will be a good deal worse than any which existed before we came.*

It was at this time that Winston Churchill set up the 1921 Cairo conference that you read about on page 108. During the conference, Gertrude warned Churchill that if Britain did not end her support for a Jewish homeland in Palestine, the Arabs in Iraq and elsewhere would never really trust them. But Churchill refused to accept this advice.

DISCUSS

Look at the list of splits and divisions in Iraq. Which of these do you think would be the biggest problem and why?
Why did Gertrude Bell say that the British should not leave Iraq?

Although she was upset by Churchill's decision on Palestine, Gertrude was delighted by the discussions on Iraq. The ideas of other advisers were rejected and she got her own way in the most important decision of all.

SOURCE 12 *British transport aeroplane patrolling the skies above Baghdad in 1920. Courtesy of the Imperial War Museum.*

Gertrude persuaded Churchill that the new king of Iraq should be Prince Feisal, who had led the Arab troops against the Turks. This was risky. Feisal was a Sunni Muslim from a distant Arab region, and most Iraqis were Shi'ite. But Feisal could trace his family line back to the Prophet Muhammad. Gertrude believed this would win the respect of both Sunnis and Shi'ites, which would allow Iraq to grow into a settled and united society.

In order to ensure that Feisal became king, Britain arrested and exiled his main nationalist opponent. Gertrude helped to fix the system so that the Iraqis did choose Feisal to rule them, and that Sunnis had more power than Shi'ites. Sure enough, Feisal was crowned king in August 1921. The next year he signed a treaty with Britain confirming British involvement for years to come – even after mandate ended.

ACTIVITY

Here is another Wackypedia entry about Gertrude. It has not understood the part that Gertrude played in making Feisal the new king of Iraq. Use pages 114–115 to help you with these two tasks:
1 Add a paragraph explaining what she really did.
2 Add any other changes or explanations that you think are needed.

In 1922 Gertrude Bell helped the Iraqi people to choose the king they wanted to rule their new nation. When he took the throne King Feisal could look forward to ruling a settled and successful nation.

◆ *'It's the making of a new world.'*

When Gertrude arrived in Baghdad in 1917, she was excited. She wrote to a friend:

'Nowhere in this war-shattered universe can we begin more speedily to make good the immense losses sustained by humanity … It's an immense opportunity … It's the making of a new world.'

This view of the Empire was shared by many British people. They truly wanted to help the people they ruled. Others said that Britain was only interested in looking after herself and that the people in her colonies would be better off without her.

Before the mandate ended in 1932, the British made many changes, especially in south and central Iraq where they had more control:

They built hospitals, schools, markets, mosques, police stations and courtrooms.

They improved drainage and water supplies to the cities.

They struck oil in the Mosul area of Iraq in 1927 and set up a British company to run the oil industry. This company and its foreign partners kept 95% of the profits. The rest helped to pay for Iraq's development.

Officers from all over the British Empire were brought to Iraq for the first few years to take charge of local districts.

They set up government ministries to look after health and education and trained Iraqis to run them.

They collected taxes once trade had revived and they used these to pay for the cost of governing Iraq.

They shared the fertile land amongst the landowners, favouring the ones who were happy to support British rule. At first they also gave them seed and cash.

They built railways between the main cities and ports – although the system was far smaller than those in India, Africa or Canada.

They repaired canals that carried river water to the fields.

They set up schools. Most schools in the Empire taught in English but these schools taught in Arabic or Kurdish, depending on the area.

They reformed the legal system. Most parts of the British Empire copied the British system of laws and courts, but in Iraq the new system was based on a Muslim model.

DISCUSS

Which things in this list suggest that Britain was trying to help Iraq prepare for self-government?

Which things in the list suggest that Britain was trying to use Iraq to serve its own interests?

◆ *Dreams and disappointments*

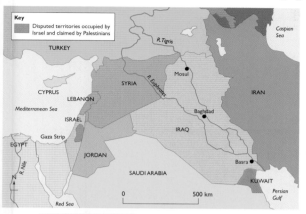

After Feisal became king in 1921, Gertrude gradually withdrew from political affairs. She set up a remarkable archaeological museum in Baghdad but she was losing her sense of purpose. In July 1926 she took an overdose of sleeping pills and died in her sleep.

Gertrude always dreamed that the Arab lands of the Middle East would become stable, peaceful states. Sadly, since her death, this has never looked possible. The two summaries below show how Gertrude's high hopes for the Middle East came to nothing.

SOURCE 15 The Middle East in 2007, showing Israel, occupied territories and the main refugee camps.

Palestine never settled. In 1948, after years of Jewish immigration, the land was partitioned between Jews and Arabs. The Arab states went to war to wipe out the new Jewish nation of Israel. But Israel won the war and took even more land. Half a million Palestinians fled their homes to live in refugee settlements. Ever since then the Palestinians have tried to regain their lands, often through politics, but also by war and terrorism. Most Muslim nations back the Palestinians and accuse the USA and Britain of favouring Israel. This Muslim mistrust of the west is exactly what Gertrude had predicted when she opposed the Balfour Declaration.

In **Iraq**, the mandate ended in 1932, but Britain kept close control of the government and profited from the oilfields. In the 1930s, oil was found in many other Arab states and British armed forces in Iraq guarded the flow of oil to the gulf.

In 1958 there was a revolution in Iraq. The new rulers broke the links with Britain. They promised to rule fairly, but Iraq has never been truly democratic and rivalries continue between Sunnis, Shi'ites and Kurds. In 1979 a dictator called Saddam Hussein took power. In 2003 western armies invaded Iraq and ended Saddam's rule, claiming that he was a threat to his own people and the world. Many Iraqis, and others, believed they were there to protect the west's oil supplies.

FINAL ACTIVITY

Here is Wackypedia's final entry about Gertrude Bell's life. It ends very weakly:

In the last six years of her life, Gertrude Bell helped Britain to rebuild Iraq after the war. She died in Baghdad in 1926. She had devoted her life in an attempt to build a great new Arab civilisation but it never developed in the way she would have wished.

Use page 116 to describe what Britain did try to do to help Iraq develop.
Look back over all the entries you have written and use them to add another paragraph that EXPLAINS why Gertrude's dream never came true.

11

END OF EMPIRE: WHAT PERSUADED THE BRITISH TO QUIT INDIA IN 1947?

Write a letter to Lord Mountbatten persuading him to grant India independence

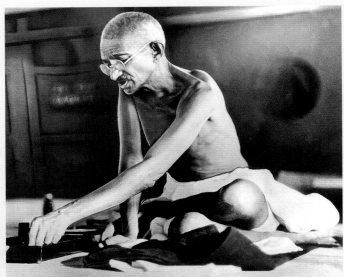

These two men look worlds apart don't they? Yet in 1947 they were drawn together to try to tackle an enormous problem: they had to decide when and how the British should finally leave India.

On the left is Lord Louis Mountbatten, the viceroy of India. He was in India to represent King George VI, emperor of India, making decisions that affected the lives of the millions of Indians living under British rule.

On the right is Mohandas Gandhi. Over the previous fifty years, Gandhi had become a representative of millions of Indians as he struggled to persuade the British that the

people of India should be allowed to rule themselves. Gandhi had recently run a campaign that called upon the British to 'Quit India'. But they were still there . . .

YOUR ENQUIRY

In this chapter you will imagine that it is February 1947. You must write a letter to Lord Mountbatten as if you are a supporter of Gandhi. You are determined that the British must leave India very soon. In your letter you will use your knowledge of India's history to persuade Mountbatten that the time has come for the British to 'Quit India'.

◆ Promises, promises . . .

The British had always publicly stated that they were not ruling India for their own benefit. As you saw in Chapter 2, the British first went to India to trade and only later took control of more and more of the land. As they became more deeply involved in ruling India, they made bold statements to show that they remained there only in order to improve it.

In 1858, following the Indian uprising of 1857 (described in Chapter 6), control of India was taken out of the hands of the East India Company. Parliament passed the Government of India Act which set up the British Raj (raj is the Indian word for rule), under a viceroy as a sort of deputy-king.

SOURCE 1 The Act stated that the British Parliament and the viceroy would:

. . . rule India for the benefit of all our subjects there.

SOURCE 2 In 1900 the viceroy of India was Lord Curzon. Here is what he said about the reason why Britain still held power over India:

If I felt that we were not working here for the good of India . . . then I would see the link that holds England and India together broken without a sigh. But it is because I believe in the future of this country and in the capacity of our own race to guide it to goals that it has never before attained, that I keep courage and press forward.

ACTIVITY

Begin your letter to Lord Mountbatten. He is an important man and you will need to choose your words carefully or he may ignore what you say. In your introduction you should remind him that in 1858 Britain promised to rule India in order to help its people. You could begin like this . . .

> February 1947
>
> To His Excellency Lord Mountbatten, viceroy of India
>
> Sir,
>
> I congratulate you on your recent appointment as His Majesty's viceroy in India. I am writing to persuade you to use your power to end the British Raj as soon as you possibly can.
>
> I will give you many reasons why the British should leave India, but first I must remind you that your people have always claimed that they took control of our land in order to help us. For example . . .

(Now use some words from the sources above and explain how they show that this **is** what the British have said.)

◆ The day of shame at Amritsar

You have already looked at the table on page 72, in which Dadabhai Naoroji listed the good and bad things about British rule as he saw it. Most historians would agree that Britain can take some credit for much of its work in India. But on 13 April 1919 there occurred the most shameful day in the history of the Raj. Here is what happened.

After the First World War (1914–18) India was very unsettled. Many Indians felt that the time had come to run their own affairs as an independent country. Angry crowds gathered all over India.

The British feared that the Indians might turn to terrorism and violence so they passed the Rowlatt Act. The Act allowed the British to imprison anyone they thought was a political trouble-maker. This just made matters worse.

The Indian people were furious. Millions took to the streets. Some demonstrated peacefully, but others did not. In the north-western city of Amritsar, mobs ran out of control, storming two banks, stealing cash and murdering then burning three white staff. An English missionary was pulled

from her bicycle and brutally assaulted.

The British were determined to restore order. On 12 April 1919 they banned all processions and public meetings in Amritsar. It did no good. The next day thousands of unarmed Indians defied this order and crowded into a large enclosed area of wasteland known as the Jallianwala Bagh. A speaker climbed onto a pile of rubble and began to read a poem of liberty. The scene was now set for the most terrible event in the history of the British Raj.

As the meeting began, there was a sound of rumbling engines and marching feet. Reginald Dyer, the soldier in charge of the British forces in Amritsar, had brought two armoured cars and about one hundred troops to teach the Indians a lesson.

Dyer ordered his soldiers to line up facing the crowd. He gave no final warning. He gave the order to fire.

The troops began shooting directly into the crowd and continued non-stop for ten minutes. The protesters panicked. They rushed towards the two exits but the gunfire cut them down. As bodies fell, people stumbled and were trampled in the crush. Some were shot as they tried to climb the high walls surrounding the Jallianwala Bagh, others threw themselves down a deep well in a desperate attempt to escape.

When it was all over, Dyer made no attempt to help the wounded. Night fell soon afterwards and no Indians were allowed on the streets after dark. The bodies lay there as wild animals came to eat their fill.

Months later, the British held an enquiry into Dyer's actions. The report established that 1600 bullets had been fired and 379 people had been killed. Dyer was forced to resign. His actions kept Amritsar under control for the short term, but, to this day, the Amritsar massacre is remembered in India as the day when the British lost their right to rule.

ACTIVITY

It is time to write the next paragraph of your letter to Lord Mountbatten. Remember that you are trying to persuade him to end British rule. Do not just write down the whole story of the Amritsar massacre. Pick out the best points to make him feel that the British lost the right to rule India by their actions at Amritsar.

You could try to answer in advance some points that Mountbatten might make about Amritsar, for example he might say:

'What happened was tragic – but we had to restore law and order.'
'It never happened again. This was not the way we usually kept order.'

◆ The Great Soul

Pressure on the British to give more power to the Indian people came from the Congress Party. This party had been founded in 1885 by educated Indians like Dadabhai Naoroji, who you read about in Chapter 6. The Party admired the British and it tried to achieve its aims by quiet discussion. Gandhi, a successful lawyer, joined the Congress Party but soon began to change its approach. His friend Jawaharlal Nehru led the party while Gandhi developed his own methods to show the British that they were in the wrong and that they must grant India independence.

Gandhi was deeply impressed by Hindu holy writings in the *Baghavad Gita*. He also admired the prophet Mohammed and this command of Jesus Christ: '*Do not resist one who is evil. But if anyone strikes you on the right cheek, turn to him the other cheek as well.*' He took these words seriously and believed that the person who never used violence was stronger than the one who did.

Gandhi turned these ideas into a non-violent way of resisting injustice. He called his method *satyagraha*, which means 'truth force'. Gandhi taught people who wanted to use satyagraha that they must accept these principles:

- *Your action must have a clear and limited aim (e.g. to end an unfair law).*
- *Before you take any action you must tell your opponents exactly what you are going to do.*
- *You must never humiliate your opponents. Your action should enlighten their minds so that they willingly do what you want.*
- *You should accept a less than perfect solution if necessary.*
- *You must never use violence, even in self defence.*
- *You must be willing to suffer and die for the cause.*

In the 1920s, Gandhi and his followers (including Nehru) applied these principles as they led many peaceful strikes, demonstrations and protests against British rule.

The British often put them in prison, but as soon as they were released they began another non-violent action. It was patience like this that made an Indian poet give Gandhi the title Mahatma, which means 'Great Soul'. But Gandhi was not just a saintly man – he was crafty as well, as he showed in his famous Salt March.

SOURCE 3 Part of a letter from Gandhi to the viceroy before his Salt March in 1930.

My ambition is no less than to convert the British people through non-violence, and to make them see the wrong they have done India. I do not seek to harm your people. I want to serve them as I serve my own.

The Salt March

You found out in Chapter 6, in the story of the Great Hedge, that the British government controlled the making and selling of salt in India – and it took half the price in tax. This was widely resented as it affected every single person. Gandhi decided to protest against the tax. He knew this would attract the support of the poorest villagers and it would show the world how unfair the British were to their Indian subjects. It would also show the British that they could not rule India without the agreement of its people.

Gandhi told the British government that he was going to walk 400 kilometres from his home village to the sea where he would break the law by making salt. He set off on 12 March 1930 and by the time he reached the sea thousands were following him. They watched as the 'Great Soul' made salt and as he quietly defied the British to arrest him once again. Gandhi made sure that there were reporters and film crews from all over the world in the crowds.

SOURCE 4 A photograph of Gandhi on the Salt March.

The British arrested Gandhi for making salt illegally, but within a few days Indians everywhere were defying the law and making their own salt. There were no massacres this time. Some rioting did break out but processions were usually non-violent as Gandhi's trained supporters acted as voluntary police. However, some protesters were killed by guards who beat them to death as they peacefully tried to occupy a salt factory.

All over the world people began to put pressure on the British government to give in. The viceroy had to make a compromise with Gandhi. He released him from prison and invited him to his palace for talks. The Raj was no longer issuing orders, it was joining in discussions.

The viceroy did not grant India independence straight away, but Gandhi did not expect that. By talking with the viceroy and with politicians in London, he helped to persuade the British to allow Indians to vote for their own Parliament of Indian politicians. The Congress Party won the elections that were held in 1937 and was soon running many – but not all – aspects of Indian life. They must have believed that complete independence was just around the corner. But the outbreak of the Second World War in 1939 changed all that.

ACTIVITY

Now write the third paragraph of your letter to persuade Lord Mountbatten that he must give India its complete independence.

◆ Remind Mountbatten how Gandhi used non-violent methods to show that the British could not rule without the agreement of the Indian people.

◆ Tell him how and why an earlier viceroy came to see that the Indians deserved more control over their lives.

◆ You could use some *rhetorical* questions, for example, 'Did Gandhi's famous Salt March teach you nothing?' or 'Can't you see that we are stronger than you?'

'Give us chaos!'

As soon as the Second World War started in September 1939, the viceroy announced that Indians would fight for the British Empire all over the world. Nehru was furious (see Source 5), but many Indians did fight loyally and thousands died during the war.

The British promised to grant independence to India as soon as possible after the war ended. The viceroy told Gandhi that it would create chaos if the British left too soon. Gandhi replied 'Then give us chaos!' He simply wanted Indians to be allowed to run their own affairs straightaway.

SOURCE 5 Nehru said of the decision to send Indians to fight in the Second World War:

There is something rotten when one man, and a foreigner and representative of a hated system, can plunge 400 million human beings into war without a slightest reference to them.

In 1942 Gandhi began the Quit India campaign of non-violent protest, but it was increasingly difficult to control the protests and there was serious rioting.

Another problem rose to the surface during the war: the age-old tension beween Hindus and Muslims. The Muslims were heavily outnumbered by Hindus and feared that they would be treated as second-class citizens once the British left. Their leader, Mohammad Ali Jinnah (see Source 7), insisted that the Muslims should be given a country of their own when independence was finally granted. He wanted India to be 'partitioned'. The longer the British stayed, the deeper they would be drawn into the conflict between Hindus and Muslims.

SOURCE 7
Mohammad Ali Jinnah.

SOURCE 6 A photograph of Indian soldiers serving in Italy in 1944.

Shortly after the war ended in 1945 Britain's new Prime Minister, Clement Attlee, promised to grant independence to India very soon. Perhaps he had been persuaded by Gandhi's non-violent protest, or perhaps he just thought India was uncontrollable. Or maybe he had noticed that Britain was no longer making anything like as much money from its trade with India as it once had.

Whatever the reason, Attlee announced that the British would leave India in June 1948 at the latest. In February 1947 he sent a new viceroy, Lord Louis Mountbatten, to organise the last days of the British Empire in India. For some Indians it could not come quickly enough!

ACTIVITY A

It is now time to write the final part of your letter to Lord Mountbatten.

Use the information on this page to persuade him that the British should leave India even earlier than June 1948. You should find plenty of reasons to give him, but be sure to use them persuasively. He won't be impressed by just a list.

◆ *Partition*

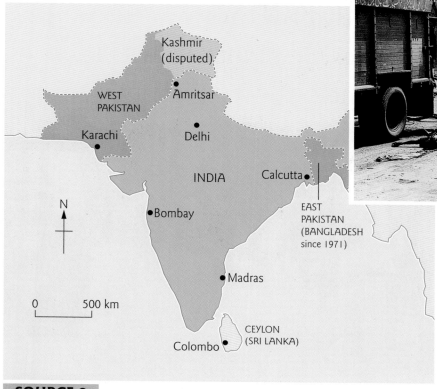

SOURCE 8 India and Pakistan, August 1947.

SOURCE 9 A photograph of victims of riots being cleared from the streets, 1947.

The story of the 'end of empire' in India has a terrible and tragic ending.

Lord Mountbatten eventually gave India her independence even earlier than Attlee had promised. The British Raj ended on 15 August 1947. But India did not remain as one single nation. Jinnah got his way and the Muslims won their own nation, called Pakistan. It occupied the two main areas of Muslim population, in north-west and north-east India.

In the months before the partition there was terrible violence between Muslims and Hindus, but even worse was to follow after partition. More than 10 million Hindus had to leave their homes and move to the right side of the new frontiers. As they flooded across the country, through towns and cities where they were not welcome, there was bloodshed on a massive scale. Muslims killed Hindus and Hindus killed Muslims.

Trainloads of people were massacred, roaming gangs attacked and murdered those who travelled on foot. At Amritsar, where the deaths of 379 people in 1919 had caused such shame, thousands now died in the streets, killed by their fellow Indians.

Gandhi did all he could to persuade Hindus to stop attacking Muslims – but this was to cost him his life. In 1948 a Hindu extremist who hated the way Gandhi had defended Muslims shot the Great Soul in cold blood. India had won her independence but she had paid a terrible price.

ACTIVITY B

Look back over your letter to Lord Mountbatten. Do you want to change it in the light of what actually happened? Did Mountbatten and Attlee get the British out of India TOO fast?

12 THE EMPIRE COMES HOME: HOW CAN WE UNCOVER THE STORIES OF BRITAIN'S COMMONWEALTH MIGRANTS?

Think of good questions for an interview with a Commonwealth migrant

SOURCE 1   Brick Lane in London's East End.

This is Brick Lane in the East End of London. Brick Lane is now a cool place to live. Luxury flats sell for more than half a million pounds. It has changed a lot over the centuries:

◆ In the seventeenth century, Protestants from France, called Huguenots, set up their weaving workshops in the lofts of Brick Lane houses. They built their own chapel in 1743.

◆ In the nineteenth century, Brick Lane became home to Irish labourers and to Jews from Russia and Eastern Europe. In 1898 the Huguenots' chapel became a synagogue.

◆ A new wave of migrants moved into Brick Lane in the 1960s. These were the Bangladeshis who came to Britain to escape the wars between India and Pakistan. Brick Lane gained many curry houses and Asian shops. In 1976 the synagogue became a mosque.

The history of Brick Lane helps us to understand something very important about Britain: WE ARE A NATION OF MIGRANTS! Over the centuries different groups of people have MIGRATED to Britain to start new lives. In recent times, many of these people have come from countries that were once part of the British Empire.

◆ African-Caribbean and Asian migrants

In 1948 the British government passed the Nationality Act. This gave United Kingdom citizenship to people from all around the COMMONWEALTH. Their British passports gave the people of the Commonwealth the right to come to Britain and stay for the rest of their lives. The politicians had opened the gate to almost 800 million people.

In the years after the war, many people from the West Indies and from the Indian sub-continent had particularly good reasons for wanting to come to Britain.

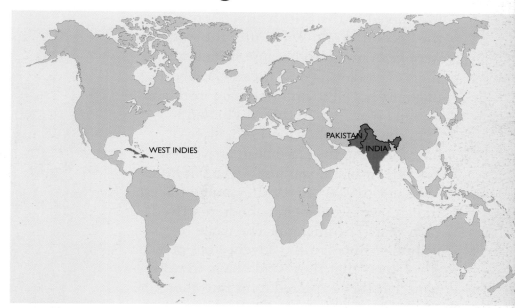

SOURCE 2   World map, showing the West Indies, India and Pakistan.

- ◆ When the ten thousand West Indian troops who had fought for Britain in the war returned to the Caribbean they found little to celebrate. In August 1944 a hurricane destroyed much of Jamaica. Jobs were hard to find because the price of sugar – the Caribbean's biggest export – was so low.
- ◆ In 1947 the British left India and created the state of Pakistan. Two million Muslims, Hindus and Sikhs were forced to leave their homes.

YOUR ENQUIRY

Many fascinating stories of individual African-Caribbean and Asian migrants who came to Britain in the three decades after the war are waiting to be uncovered. All you have to do is some oral history research. Oral history is what people say about their past experiences. To be a good oral historian you need to do some background research. You also need to think hard about the questions you ask. In this enquiry you will put together a set of good questions to interview either an African-Caribbean or an Asian migrant about their experiences of coming to Britain in the decades after the Second World War.

African-Caribbean migrants

For the men in this photograph, 22 June 1948 was a very special day. The long sea voyage from the West Indies was over. The *SS Empire Windrush* had finally landed in Britain. Many of the 492 Jamaicans on board had served in the British armed forces during the Second World War. After the war, they were keen to return because Britain was short of workers. The African-Caribbean migrants hoped to find well-paid work and to build new lives in the 'Motherland'.

In the years following 1948, more migrants from the Caribbean arrived in Britain. At first it was just a few, but from 1955 until 1962, tens of thousands of West Indian men, women and children arrived each year. The migrants who came to Britain were brave and adventurous people. They knew that they would have to work hard, but they expected to fit into the British way of life quite easily. After all, the West Indians spoke good English; they loved football and cricket; most of them were Christians; they knew a lot about Britain from their lessons at school.

In June 1948, newspapers and cinema newsreels gave the African-Caribbean migrants a warm welcome. But the warm welcome soon turned cold. As they began to settle in Britain, the West Indians faced PREJUDICE and racism. In the 1950s many white British people had never met a black person. They were struggling to build their own lives after the war, and resented the new black migrants. As large numbers of migrants arrived, many white people began to see the African-Caribbean population as a threat.

SOURCE 3 Migrants waiting to disembark from the *SS Empire Windrush*, 22 June 1948.

DISCUSS

What can you find out about the African-Caribbean migrants from the photograph in Source 3?

Many of these Jamaicans are now in their 70s and 80s. If you were to interview one of them about their life in the West Indies, their journey on the Windrush and their arrival in Britain in June 1948, what questions would you want to ask?

◆ Somewhere to live

Once off the ships, the African-Caribbean migrants travelled to cities across Britain by train. How strange this country seemed! When they first saw rows of brick houses with chimneys, many migrants thought that the houses must be factories.

Wartime bomb damage meant that houses in Britain were in short supply. It was especially hard for West Indians to find a place to live. There was almost no social housing and many private landlords displayed signs saying 'No Blacks' or 'No Coloured Men'.

Many African-Caribbean migrants went to areas where people from their own island had already settled. These were often the poorest parts of cities where rents were cheaper: Jamaicans went to Brixton or Wolverhampton; the Guyanese lived mainly in Tottenham in London, or Moss Side in Manchester; the Trinidadians went to Notting Hill in London. If migrants tried to buy or rent a home in a better area, they could be abused or attacked. Most, therefore, stayed in the 'black areas' of Britain's cities.

◆ Finding a job

The African-Caribbean migrants came from a range of backgrounds. Many were professionals, or skilled workers such as teachers, engineers and nurses. Others were unskilled or semi-skilled: farmers or tradesmen without qualifications or training. Some British employers offered the migrants reasonably paid work. But many employers refused to accept African-Caribbean workers. Skilled migrants were often forced to settle for unskilled and low-paid work, such as night-shift work in factories, labouring on building sites or sweeping the streets.

When looking for a job, migrants often faced prejudice and racism from Britain's white population. Some white British people refused to work with African-Caribbean migrants. Companies and trade unions often discriminated against them. In Bristol, for example, the bus company refused to take on West Indian workers until a boycott of its buses by Bristol's black community forced a change of policy. It was not until the 1960s that the British government introduced laws against discrimination at work. Only then did African-Caribbean workers begin to be treated fairly.

ACTIVITY

Remember that your challenge in this enquiry is to find out about the individual experiences of a Commonwealth migrant in the 1950s and 1960s. Now you have some background knowledge of the early experiences of the African-Caribbean community, think of five good questions that would help an African-Caribbean migrant to talk about their early experiences in Britain.

◆ The 1958 Notting Hill riots

By 1958, 113,000 West Indians were living in Britain. As unemployment began to rise, Caribbean people faced growing resentment from parts of Britain's white population. In the late 1950s this resentment was fuelled by politicians like Sir Oswald Mosley who held racist meetings in East and West London. Mosley set up an office in the Notting Hill area of London and produced leaflets encouraging white British people to 'Protect Your Jobs', 'Stop Coloured Immigration', and 'Act Now'. Some of Britain's Teddy Boys – young men who wore Edwardian-style clothes and enjoyed rock and roll music – were only too happy to take action. They were looking for trouble, and Britain's migrant community made a good target.

During August 1958, the African-Caribbean population of Notting Hill faced racist attacks on a daily basis. Crowds of white people shouted racial abuse at them when they walked down the street. Sometimes groups of racists chased them. One Jamaican was shot in the leg. Some Caribbean families had petrol bombs thrown at their houses. Many West Indian families must have wondered why they had ever come to Britain.

At the end of August things turned very nasty. Just before midnight on 30 August, a crowd of around 200 white racists attacked African-Caribbean houses. One house was set alight. The next night, a larger mob of 600, armed with knives, bottles and crowbars, attacked black people in their homes. The police did little to stop the violence. On the third day, young black people decided to fight back. They knew what was coming and made their own petrol bombs. This time, the police moved in as hundreds of young black and white men fought on the streets of Notting Hill.

By the end of September, the situation had calmed down. But the 1958 riot in Notting Hill marked a turning point for Britain's Commonwealth migrants. Some British politicians began to argue for stricter controls on immigration. In 1962 the government introduced an Immigration Act which limited Commonwealth immigration. Now people in the Commonwealth needed a work permit before they could come to Britain. The politicians were closing the gate to Commonwealth migrants.

DISCUSS

What questions would you want to ask a member of the African-Caribbean community who remembers the Notting Hill riot?

SOURCE 4 The Notting Hill riot.

◆ The beginnings of Black British identity

In the years after 1958, the African-Caribbean community began to create a more powerful identity in Britain. African-Caribbean people began to express themselves in new and creative ways. They drew on their own heritage and combined this with their experiences of living in the UK. The result was an identity which we now call Black British.

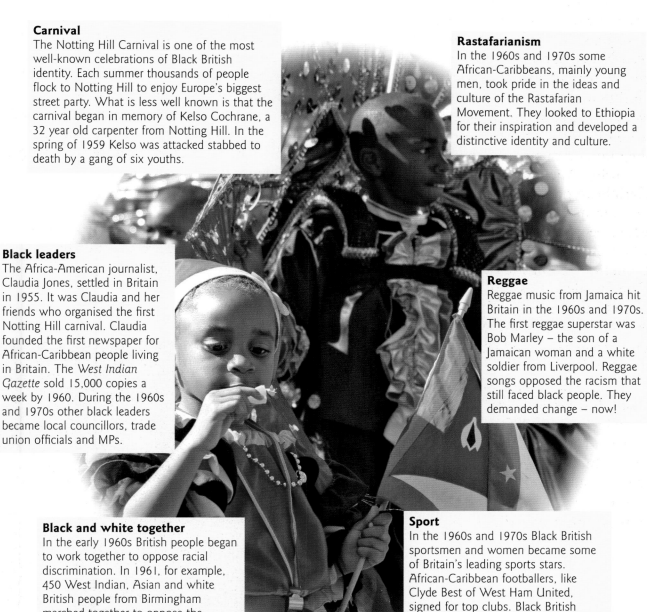

Carnival
The Notting Hill Carnival is one of the most well-known celebrations of Black British identity. Each summer thousands of people flock to Notting Hill to enjoy Europe's biggest street party. What is less well known is that the carnival began in memory of Kelso Cochrane, a 32 year old carpenter from Notting Hill. In the spring of 1959 Kelso was attacked stabbed to death by a gang of six youths.

Rastafarianism
In the 1960s and 1970s some African-Caribbeans, mainly young men, took pride in the ideas and culture of the Rastafarian Movement. They looked to Ethiopia for their inspiration and developed a distinctive identity and culture.

Black leaders
The Africa-American journalist, Claudia Jones, settled in Britain in 1955. It was Claudia and her friends who organised the first Notting Hill carnival. Claudia founded the first newspaper for African-Caribbean people living in Britain. The *West Indian Gazette* sold 15,000 copies a week by 1960. During the 1960s and 1970s other black leaders became local councillors, trade union officials and MPs.

Reggae
Reggae music from Jamaica hit Britain in the 1960s and 1970s. The first reggae superstar was Bob Marley – the son of a Jamaican woman and a white soldier from Liverpool. Reggae songs opposed the racism that still faced black people. They demanded change – now!

Black and white together
In the early 1960s British people began to work together to oppose racial discrimination. In 1961, for example, 450 West Indian, Asian and white British people from Birmingham marched together to oppose the Commonwealth Immigration Bill.

Sport
In the 1960s and 1970s Black British sportsmen and women became some of Britain's leading sports stars. African-Caribbean footballers, like Clyde Best of West Ham United, signed for top clubs. Black British athletes won medals for Britain at the Commonwealth and Olympic games.

Asian migrants

Mohindra Chowdhry was born into a Sikh family in India in 1941. Mohindra's family owned a construction company and were very rich. They lived in a large house with a swimming pool. In 1947, the British partitioned India and created the new state of Pakistan. Mohindra's family found themselves on the wrong side of the border. This was a time of great violence in India and the Chowdhrys were afraid that they would be murdered. They left their beautiful house and never saw it again. Mohindra's family lived in a tent as refugees.

In 1962, after the death of his mother, Mohindra came to Britain. He lived in Bristol, working at Avonmouth Docks during the day and studying engineering in the evening. Mohindra sent most of the money he earned to his father in India.

DISCUSS

Think of three good questions to ask Mohindra about his experiences of migration.

During British rule in India many Asians came to live in Britain. But it was after the partition of India in 1947 that a new pattern of Asian migration began. Millions of Hindus, Muslims and Sikhs, like Mohindra Chowdry, were made homeless when India was partitioned. India and Pakistan were poor countries and many young men thought that they could earn money to support their families if they moved to Britain.

Few Asian migrants planned to stay in Britain for the rest of their lives, but many eventually settled here and were joined by their families. In 1962 there was a huge increase in migration from India as people tried to move to Britain before the Commonwealth Immigration Act restricted the number of migrants. In the late 1960s and early 1970s there was another surge of Asian immigration, this time from East Africa. Asians had settled in East Africa during British rule, but, after independence, rulers in Kenya and Uganda forced the Asians to leave.

SOURCE 5 Asian migrants working in a factory.

Finding a job

The Asian migrants came from a variety of backgrounds. Some were professionals such as doctors who came to work in Britain's new National Health Service. However, many of the doctors, dentists, teachers and lawyers who came to Britain discovered that their Indian qualifications were not accepted. One dentist, for example, was forced to become a bus conductor.

Most Asian migrants were unskilled workers who found jobs in one of Britain's booming industries. They worked in textile factories in Lancashire and Yorkshire, in steel works in Sheffield or iron foundries in the Midlands. Many Indian and Pakistani men worked night shifts, because these were unpopular with white British workers.

Making a new life

Source 6 shows us that migration often causes sadness and pain. Very few Asian migrants who came to Britain after 1947 could afford to bring their families with them. Most left their families with relatives until they had earned enough money to return or to send for them. In the 1960s, wives and children began to join their husbands and fathers in Britain. For Asian women, coming from large extended families in rural areas and often speaking little English, life in Britain could be isolated and lonely. At school, Asian children had to quickly get used to English food, language and people.

SOURCE 6 A family farewell in India.

ACTIVITY

Now you have some background information about Asian migration to Britain in the decades after the Second World War, think of three good questions to ask an Asian migrant who came to this country in this period.

◆ Discrimination and violence

Asian migrants often faced ignorance and discrimination from white Britons. One migrant, who arrived in Britain in 1946, described a confrontation with a local man:

When I first arrived, the local people generally didn't like us blacks. Once I remember being confronted by a white man telling me 'You blacks are good for nothing. You come over here, take our jobs and we don't like you.' I told him that it was my country too. I had fought for it and if we had been late in getting to the battlefront this country would have been in the hands of the Germans. I told him not to give me any trouble as I had sacrificed a lot for this country. The man apologised at the end saying he didn't know.

By the 1960s the British government recognised that something had to be done about race relations. It passed Race Relations Acts in 1965, 1968 and 1976. These made discrimination illegal. But Britain's migrant communities still faced hostility and sometimes violence. In the 1970s, the Bengali community of East London were harassed by the National Front and their allies. Stones were thrown through windows and gangs of racists attacked people in the streets. Then, in May 1978, Altab Ali, a Bangladeshi garment worker, was murdered. Seven thousand people marched with Altab's coffin from the site of his murder to 10 Downing Street. The photo in Source 7 shows the park in London that was named after him.

SOURCE 7 Altab Ali park

> **DISCUSS**
>
> How could you phrase a good question about the discrimination and violence faced by the Asian community?

◆ The beginnings of Asian British identity

During the 1960s and 1970s, Britain's Asian population grew in size, wealth and confidence. In this period we see the beginnings of an Asian British identity which helps to make Britain such a dynamic and rich country today.

ACTIVITY

Read about some of the ways in which Asian British identity was created. Think of five good interview questions about the beginnings of Asian British identity in the 1960s and 70s.

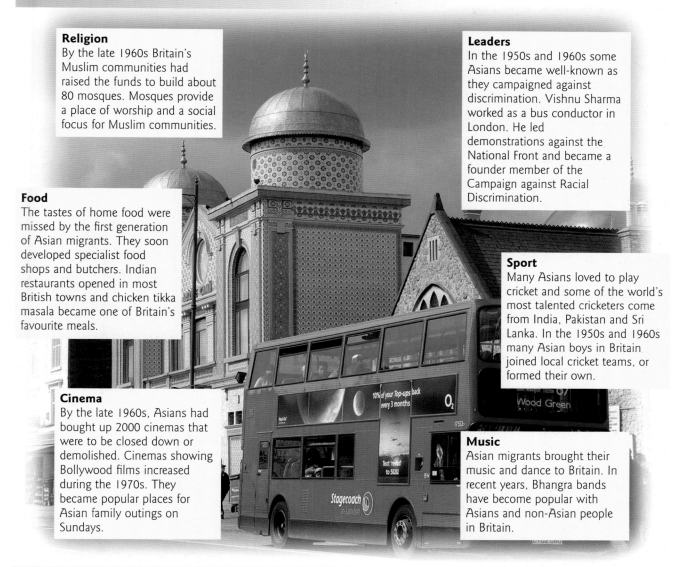

Religion
By the late 1960s Britain's Muslim communities had raised the funds to build about 80 mosques. Mosques provide a place of worship and a social focus for Muslim communities.

Food
The tastes of home food were missed by the first generation of Asian migrants. They soon developed specialist food shops and butchers. Indian restaurants opened in most British towns and chicken tikka masala became one of Britain's favourite meals.

Cinema
By the late 1960s, Asians had bought up 2000 cinemas that were to be closed down or demolished. Cinemas showing Bollywood films increased during the 1970s. They became popular places for Asian family outings on Sundays.

Leaders
In the 1950s and 1960s some Asians became well-known as they campaigned against discrimination. Vishnu Sharma worked as a bus conductor in London. He led demonstrations against the National Front and became a founder member of the Campaign against Racial Discrimination.

Sport
Many Asians loved to play cricket and some of the world's most talented cricketers come from India, Pakistan and Sri Lanka. In the 1950s and 1960s many Asian boys in Britain joined local cricket teams, or formed their own.

Music
Asian migrants brought their music and dance to Britain. In recent years, Bhangra bands have become popular with Asians and non-Asian people in Britain.

FINAL ACTIVITY

You have found out a lot about the experiences of Britain's Commonwealth migrants. It will be interesting to find out how individual migrants fit into this bigger picture.

It is now time to put together the questions for your oral history interview with a Caribbean or an Asian migrant to Britain. Use the questions you have drafted to put together a questionnaire of eight to ten questions to use in your interview. Think carefully about:

◆ which aspects of the migrant experience your questions will try to uncover
◆ the sequence of your questions
◆ the way you phrase your questions to get the fullest possible answers.

Maybe you can do a real interview with a Commonwealth migrant.

CONCLUSION: HOW DO YOU SEE THE BRITISH EMPIRE?

Challenge the authors – and challenge yourself!

Source 1 shows the world today with British territory shown in red. We've enjoyed producing this book and following the rise and fall of the British Empire. But it has been a difficult task! The British Empire was so huge; it lasted for such a long time; it included so many different people, ideas and events.

Deciding what to leave out and what to put in our textbook has been a headache. We've tried to include the things that we think were most important to people in the British Empire – both the rulers and the ruled. We've also tried to produce a balanced and fair book. It took lots of discussion amongst ourselves to settle on the topics you see in this book. There were some heated arguments!

> I want to have a chapter on sport in the Empire.

> We can't leave out the Pilgrim Fathers, surely?

> We should have had more examples of how people resisted empire and won independence!

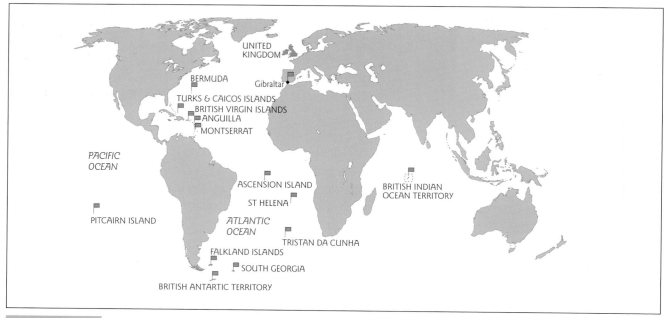

SOURCE 1 Map of the world today, with British territory shown in red.

We know that this textbook is just our interpretation of the British Empire. Lots of people might want to criticise our interpretation. They might have very different ideas about what to include in a textbook on the British Empire.

How could you leave out some of the great heroes of the British Empire like General Gordon and Cecil Rhodes?

Why didn't you have a separate enquiry on the American Revolution? It was one of the most important turning points in the history of the British Empire.

You should have included a separate enquiry on Tasmania. What the British did there was terrible!

Why haven't you written at least one chapter through the eyes of the people they ruled?

Your book is nearly all about men. Where are the women?

What about the Opium Wars: smashing into China to force them to buy opium from the British?

We are pleased that people have such strong views about our textbook and that it stirs up new thoughts and feelings. At least it shows that:

◆ history is complicated

◆ people care about history

◆ history is worth arguing about.

◆ history affects the way we see the world around us.
   Turn the page and test this out!

◆ Your final challenge

Here is the street that you saw at the start of this book
(pages 2–3). This time a few more details have been
revealed.

Look carefully at the street scene. How many details can
you find that are linked in some way to the British Empire?
We think you may be able to find at least fifteen, and maybe

more. See if you can connect them to particular stories in this book.

Of course this is just an artist's picture. The important thing is to be aware of how the British Empire has shaped your REAL world and the way you live in it.

History is not dead and gone – it's all around us!

Glossary

artillery a section of the army that uses large guns

bilges the lowest part of the inside of a ship

berth a fixed bunk on a ship

bush a wild, uncultivated area of land in Australia

cat o' nine tails a rope whip with nine knotted lashes used for flogging people

cauterise to burn a wound in order to stop bleeding

civilisation a people or nation with a highly organised system of social development

colonists the people living in a colony

colony an area of land controlled and inhabited by people from another country

Commonwealth an association made up of the United Kingdom and states that were previously part of the British Empire

conscription compulsory service in the armed forces

deposed removed from power

dysentery a serious disease affecting the intestines

empire a large group of countries ruled by one power

exploited to be taken advantage of for someone else's benefit

famine severe food shortage, causing widespread hunger and deaths

independence when a country becomes self-governing

leprosy infectious disease, causing damage to skin, nerves, limbs and eyes

migration the movement of people from one country to another

minaret a tower connected to a mosque, from where worshippers are called to prayer

musket a light gun supported on the shoulder

partition splitting a country into two or more parts

patriotic having a strong loyalty to one's country

penal punishment or the means of administering it

pitch a dark sticky substance used for sealing the seams of ships

plantations initially used to describe English and Scottish settlements created in the seventeenth century out of land taken from Irish in Ulster. Later used to describe estates in the colonies growing a single crop for export, often using slave labour

prejudice pre-judging e.g. treating someone differently because you believe they are different to yourself

provisions stores of food and drink taken on a voyage

scurvy a disease caused by a lack of vitamin C, causing bleeding gums and the opening of previously healed wounds

serfdom a system where some of the people are oppressed and forced to work for others

shareholders people who own shares in a company

shrapnel fragments of a bomb blown out by an explosion

soothsayers people who can foresee the future and divine the truth

yaws a skin disease causing large red swellings

◆ Index

THIS IS HISTORY!

◆ Titles in the series

Pupil's Books (PB) and Teacher's Resource Books (TRB) are available for all titles.

Write Your Own Roman Story	PB 0 7195 7717 9	TRB 0 7195 7718 7
The Norman Conquest	PB 0 7195 8555 4	TRB 0 7195 8556 2
King John	PB 0 7195 8539 2	TRB 0 7195 8540 6
Lost in Time	PB 0 7195 8557 0	TRB 0 7195 8558 9
'King' Cromwell?	PB 0 7195 8559 7	TRB 0 7195 8560 0
The Impact of Empire	PB 0 7195 8561 9	TRB 0 7195 8562 7
Dying for the Vote	PB 0 7195 8563 5	TRB 0 7195 8564 3
The Trenches	PB 0 7195 8565 1	TRB 0 7195 8566 X
The Holocaust	PB 0 7195 7709 8	TRB 0 7195 7710 1
The Twentieth Century	PB 0 7195 7711 X	TRB 0 7195 7712 8

◆ Acknowledgements

The Publishers would like to thank the following for permission to reproduce copyright material:

Photo credits
pp. 4, 6 and 7 National Portrait Gallery, London; **p. 11** The Art Archive / British Museum / Harper Collins Publishers; **p. 13** The Art Archive / British Museum / Eileen Tweedy; **p. 15** The British Museum/Heritage Images; **p. 18** By permission of the British Library; **p. 20** The British Library/ Heritage Images; **p. 24** Admiral Sir Edward Hawke defeating Admiral M. de Conflans in the Bay of Biscay, Luny, Thomas (1759-1837) / Private Collection, / The Bridgeman Art Library; **pp. 26 and 37** National Portrait Gallery, London; **pp. 28–29** The Art Archive / General Wolfe Museum Quebec House / Eileen Tweedy; **p. 30** National Gallery of Canada, Ottawa; **pp. 32 and 37** National Trust Photographic Library / John Hammond; **p. 33** The Battle of Arcot by Doughty, C.L. (1913-85) Private Collection / © Look and Learn / The Bridgeman Art Library; **p. 34** By permission of the British Library; **p. 33** The Battle of Arcot by Doughty, C.L. (1913-85) Private Collection / © Look and Learn / The Bridgeman Art Library (detail); **p. 36** National Portrait Gallery, London; **p. 38** Slaves on the West Coast of Africa, c.1833 (oil on canvas), Biard, Francois Auguste (1798-1882) / © Wilberforce House, Hull City Museums and Art Galleries, UK / The Bridgeman Art Library; **p. 40** View of the Southwell Frigate Trading on the Coast of Africa, c.1760 (pen & ink and wash), Pocock, Nicholas (1741–1821) / © Bristol City Museum and Art Gallery, UK / The Bridgeman Art Library; **p. 42** Slaves Fell the Ripe Sugar, Antigua, 1823 (print), Clark, William (fl.1823) / British Library, London, UK, © British Library Board. All Rights Reserved / The Bridgeman Art Library; **p. 43** *t* The Crusher Squeezes Juice from the Cane, Antigua, 1823 (print), Clark, William (fl.1823) / British Library, London, UK, © British Library Board. All Rights Reserved / The Bridgeman Art Library, *b* Slaves Ladle Steaming Juice from Vat to Vat, Antigua, 1823 (print), Clark, William (fl.1823) / British Library, London, UK, © British Library Board. All Rights Reserved / The Bridgeman Art Library; **p. 46** © Walker Art Gallery, National Museums Liverpool; **p. 47** National Gallery of Canada, Ottawa; **p. 49** © Christie's Images Ltd; **p. 50** *t* © Peter M Fisher/Corbis, *b* Captain Arthur Phillip (1738-1814) (engraving) (b/w photo), English School, (19th century) / Private Collection, / The Bridgeman Art Library; **p. 51** The Natural History Museum, London; **p. 52** Prison Ship in Portsmouth Harbour: Convicts Going on Board, 1828 (engraving) (b/w photo), Cooke, Edward William (1811–80) / Private Collection, / The Bridgeman Art Library; **p. 53** Mary Evans Picture Library; **p. 54** *t* The Entrance of Port Jackson, and part of the town of Sydney in New South Wales, left section of panoramic view, c.1821 (aquatint), Taylor, Major James (early 19th century) (after) / Mitchell Library, State Library of New South Wales, / The Bridgeman Art Library, *b* Earle, Augustus: View from the summit of Mount York, looking towards Bathurst Plains, convicts breaking stones, N. S. Wales, PIC T61 NK 12/23 CON1207 LOC Box A32; National Library of Australia, Canberra;

*"Round the house
and mind the dresser."
With love for Mum and Dad.*

First published 1997 by Walker Books Ltd
87 Vauxhall Walk, London SE11 5HJ

This edition published 1999

2 4 6 8 10 9 7 5 3 1

© 1997 Patricia Casey

This book has been typeset in Gill Sans.

Printed in Singapore

British Library Cataloguing in Publication Data
A catalogue record for this book is
available from the British Library.

ISBN 0-7445-6341-0

Beep! Beep! Oink! Oink!
Animals in the City

Patricia Casey

WALKER BOOKS
AND SUBSIDIARIES
LONDON · BOSTON · SYDNEY

Pit-pat, pit-pat. Look who's walking on the pavement with the people! **Pigeons!**

They're looking for **food.** They know there's always food where there are people. That's why lots of **animals** like living in the **city.** You see them in all sorts of places. The city is their **home.**

SCREEEEECCH! Can you hear the **seagulls? RAFF! RAFF!** Can you hear a **dog** giving a boy a fast rollerskate ride?

If you listen carefully, you can hear animals wherever you go. Their **sounds** are part of the city.

Caw, caw! Can you hear the **crows** in the park?

Let's go see what we can find...

Wherever you look in the city, down at the ground ...

Can you see a **sparrow**
nestling in Smokey's
warm, snug pocket?
Smokey is feeding it
with **breadcrumbs.**

Seagulls and **pigeons** love the city because it is full of **tall** places to perch, like ...

arms and heads,

bus stops, parking meters, lampposts,

walls, hot-dog stands,

and even TIGERS!

This **chicken** lives in a city **back garden.**
One morning Mrs Lambert came back from the shops,
and there she was – sitting in the **plum tree!**
Mrs Lambert named her **Clare.**

Clare stayed. She lays lots of **eggs,**
and Mrs Lambert makes
delicious **omelettes** and **cakes**
and **ice-cream** with them.

Mr Coller found this little **terrier dog** wandering about alone in a city street. His owner had abandoned him. No one wanted him but Mr Coller did.

He took him home and named him **Lucky.**
But really he thinks **he's** the lucky one.
Lucky is such a good friend to Mr Coller...

Every day he takes Mr Coller out for walks.

He sniffs the way the wind is blowing ...

and that's the way they go!

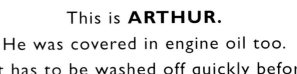
This is **ARTHUR.**
He was covered in engine oil too.
(It has to be washed off quickly before
the cats try to lick themselves clean.
Butter is used to break it down.
Then they have lots of washes
in baby shampoo.)

OLIVE got her name because
she was found covered in oil.
Not olive oil – engine oil.
Engine oil is a hazard
if you're a city cat.

CINDY
came because
she was run
over by a car.
She only has
three legs.
She can run
and jump,
but she avoids
fights because
if she uses
her front paw
she just
topples over!

BILL was in
a road accident.
Two inches had to be
taken off the tip
of his tail.

ANGUS
is so tatty no one
would give him a home!

Lost or stray city cats are looked after at CAT SANCTUARIES.

ROWAN was brought in by a school teacher. He had been living in the school playground and the children had been feeding him.

ZEBEDEE was half wild. He was found stuck up a tree.

ROSE was owned by an old lady who died. She loves jumpers – even if you're wearing them!

OLLIE was left on the doorstep in a cardboard box.

You can come and visit the cats in cat sanctuaries. They love visitors. They climb all over you!

This is **Poppy.** She is on her way to a **grooming parlour.** That's where dogs in the city get their hair cut.

Can you guess what
kind of **dog** she is?
It's hard to tell now.
She's so **shaggy!**

Poppy looks **worried.**
She knows what's
coming **next...**

Uh-oh! Here we go.

1. A trim.

2. A shower.

4. A spell in the drying cupboard.

5. A brushing to get rid of the knots.

3. A blow dry.

6. A toenail clipping and one final fancy bit of grooming.

Can you guess yet what kind of dog Poppy is?

She's a POODLE!

Phew!

Over at last,
thinks Poppy.

(Till the next time.)

City animals like
to get about – it's
quicker to go
on wheels!

Who's that glamorous lady riding in that car?

Oh! She's an Afghan hound!

And who are these other city-riders?

A ferret on a bus!

A dachshund on a bicycle!

A puppy in a shopping trolley!

A mouse on an underground train!

A kitten in a pram!

A goose on a skateboard!

I have three cats, but **MUSTARD** is my favourite. He's blind, but he has lovely long whiskers and he can feel where he is with them.

Old English sheepdogs are very hairy. We keep **CHARLIE'S** coat short so he can see where he's going!

My sister calls my mouse **BACON**, but I call him **SAUSAGE.**

Hello, Beautiful! Give us a kiss!

TOFFEE has pointy ears and he likes to pretend he's a gremlin! He's king in my house.

The waiting-room at the

Pepper, come here. NO!

Mummy!

MUTTLEY'S allergic to fleas.

My cat's called KISMIC. A car hurt his leg. I hope the vet can fix it 'cos he loves jumping on my mum's bed. I love him very much.

BUFFER loves pizza and he knows what you're thinking. He was real pretty when he was a puppy. Look at him now!

BENJI is thirteen years old. I clean his teeth with a toothbrush.

vet's is a good place to meet city pets.

Meggy is a "**wedding-car cat**".
She sleeps in a city **garage** that
belongs to Mr and Mrs McClelland.
She shares it with the
limousines they hire out.

The night before a **wedding,**
Mr and Mrs McClelland **wash**
and **polish** and **decorate**
one of the cars with
ribbons and flowers.

It looks
beautiful!

PU

But when they come back in the morning, they find Meggy has added her own **finishing touches.**

Oh dear!
They have to start all over again!

(They have some **other** names for Meggy when this happens!)

Buildings are like beds for the **starlings**. At dusk,
they fly in to roost on city **roofs** and **ledges** and **sills**.

While the starlings sleep, other animals wake up.

Owls,

hungry foxes,

bats,

and ravenous rats.

Moths dance under the streetlights.

At dawn, the **squirrels** get up. (They make good alarm clocks.) And the starlings fly off for another city day.

Gloria is a **pig** who lives on a **farm** in the city. When she was a **tiny baby** she was found beside a motorway – all alone, without her mother. Mr Ower, the farmer, and his family did everything to make sure she stayed alive.

Goat's milk is best for a lost piglet.

They fed her with it from a baby's bottle every two hours, night and day.

They put her in a cardboard box in the kitchen,

and kept her warm with a heat lamp.

Soon she got better and came out to explore.

She liked biting shoes and ankles and toes.

And she met Jason the Alsatian. When she squealed he looked at her with great concern.

SQUEAL
SQUEAL
SQUEAL
SQUEAL
SQUEAL
SQUEAL //
SQUEAL
SQUEAL
eeeeeekk
SQUEAL

Jason was like a mother to Gloria. He **licked** her a lot, as though she were his **puppy.**

Gloria began to grow quickly. She **grew** and **grew** and **grew…**

Look how glorious **Gloria** is now!
She weighs over **a hundred kilos.**
She does not live in the **kitchen** any more.
She has a **pen** of her own.

CLIP-CLOP! CLIP-CLOP!

There's a **parade** in the city and here
are the **horses,** carrying the children in **fancy dress.**

This is **Storm.**
He's carrying two **snowmen.** He **wishes** they would
just melt. The parade makes him so **fed up!**

This is **Lady.**
She's dressed like a **reindeer,** but of course,
she's a **horse!** She **loves** the parade.

GALLOPY-GALLOP!
Sounds like **thunder!**

Storm is **kicking** up a **storm**.
And look, one of the snowmen has
dropped his snowflakes. It's **snowing!**
Storm **loves** the parade now, too!

Sammy **the rabbit** lives in a hutch in the **playground**

I give her ham and cake and grass and leaves and water.

He's very very very soft and delicate. You can feel his bones when you stroke him.

When you pick her up she tries to wriggle away and hide under her house.

She's a **she**, not a **he**, **silly**.

of a city school. The children are her **friends.**

Caw, caw!
Here are all
the **crows**
in the **park.**

They love it at **lunchtime.** Crows are always **hungry.**

They **strut** and **march** about and peck up **titbits.**

Not everyone likes to share his lunch with the **crow crowd...**

MORE WALKER PAPERBACKS
For You to Enjoy

MY CAT JACK
by Patricia Casey

"This beautiful book is simply a celebration of the animal yawning,
stretching, scratching, purring and washing, with some of the best drawings
of a cat I have ever seen." *Anthony Browne, The Financial Times*

0-7445-4360-6   £4.99

TOWN PARROT
by Penelope Bennett/Sue Heap

"A small masterpiece, superbly crafted, telling the story of an urban parrot…
The illustrations in soft watercolour are sensitive and accurate…
A must for primary classrooms." *The School Librarian*

0-7445-4727-X   £4.99

A RUINED HOUSE
by Mick Manning

In the ruined house all kinds of creatures make their home…

"A treasure hunt, a natural history lesson and a detective story all rolled into one,
which should inspire its readers to regard the outwardly unpromising features of their own
environment with fresh curiosity… A compulsive read." *Junior Education*

0-7445-4728-8   £4.99